EASY BEANS

Fast and delicious bean, pea and lentil recipes

Trish Ross and Jacquie Trafford

BIG BEAN PUBLISHING

Big Bean Publishing
Suite 201-1508 Mariners Walk
Vancouver, British Columbia
Canada V6J 4X9

CANADIAN CATALOGUING IN PUBLICATION DATA

Ross, Trish   Trafford, Jacquie
        Easy Beans

ISBN 0-9698162-0-0

1. Cookery (Beans) 2. Cookery (Peas) 3. Cookery (Lentils)

TX803.B4R68 1996 641.6565   C96-910818-4

Text design and typesetting, Stubblejumper Communications
Text illustrations, Neil Thacker
Cover design, Val Speidel
Cover photograph, Clinton Hussey
Food stylist, Wayne Palmer-Haenisch

Printed and bound in Canada
Printed on acid-free paper

Contents

Thanks Everyone

To all our friends, relatives and co-workers who have shared their recipes and tasted more bean dishes this past year than they ever thought they would eat in a lifetime, and still encouraged us to keep cooking.

To Moira McLeod, whose computer expertise and layout skills made the splattered, dog-earred recipes readable and professional.

And, to Neil Thacker whose graphic artistry made personalities of the normally humble bean.

Why We Did It

*I*t was time for a change – time to try new menus – time for healthful, tasty, economical meals. Beans were the answer but where were the cookbooks? Shelves of "how to's" for chicken and pasta abounded but pitifully few for the exotic bean.

And so, over lunch it began. Write a cookbook that makes beans as mainstream and quick to prepare as pasta. One that is so simple and clear and filled with such delicious recipes that even the most "bean challenged" of cooks would be enticed.

A year and hundreds of pounds of beans later, <u>Easy Beans</u> is a reality. We hope you will enjoy the results and "spill the beans" to all your friends.

Personal Bits:

Jacquie lives on Shuswap Lake in B.C.'s interior.

Trish is a short stroll from Granville Island in Vancouver, B.C.

Both have three children and both have been cooking and entertaining for more years than they care to reveal.

Three Cheers for Beans

*L*egumes *(beans, peas and lentils) are not only versatile, easy to cook and economical, they are extremely good for you.*

They are:

- high in fibre
- high in protein
- rich in complex carbohydrates
- low in fat (except soy beans)
- low in sodium
- rich in minerals:
    - high in potassium, phosphorous
    - moderate amounts of calcium and iron
- good source of B vitamins, thiamin, niacin and folic acid

More About Fibre:

- Beans, peas and lentils contain soluble and unsoluble fibre.
- It is thought that the high fibre, low fat content of legumes may lower the incidence of heart disease.

Soluble Fibre:

- Studies have shown that soluble fibre
    - reduces cholesterol levels
    - delays entry of sugar into the intestines (good for diabetics).

Insoluble fibre:

■ Remedies constipation.

More About Protein:

■ Beans, peas and lentils combined with grains are the prime protein source in many countries of the world.

■ They have the highest concentration of vegetable protein (twice that of grains).

■ They are an incomplete protein but when combined with grain, seeds or nuts, which are also incomplete, they make a complete protein. Simplistically put, 1/2 +1/2 = 1 (e.g. Vegetarian Lasagna).

■ It has been found that the body uses an incomplete protein more efficiently when it is teamed with a complete protein such as dairy products, eggs, meat or fish (e.g. Feta Garbanzo Salad).

Extra Bonuses:

■ Legumes are gluten-free. This makes them ideal for a celiac diet.

■ Helpful for weight control. Legumes take a long time to digest so suppress appetite. They are also low in fat.

■ There is considerable evidence that regular bean eaters have lower blood pressure.

According to Canada's Food Guide to Healthy Eating:

■ The intake of complex carbohydrates from a variety of sources should include dried peas, beans and lentils.

■ A good way to cut fat is to frequently choose leaner meats, poultry and fish as well as dried peas, beans and lentils.

So, You can see they really are GOOD FOR YOU!

Welcome to the World of Beans

*P*ulses??? Legumes??? *You might see these two names when you are looking for, or reading about beans, peas and lentils. "Pulses" are the dried edible seeds of the legume plant. "Legumes" is a commonly used term to describe beans, peas and lentils as a group.*

Three Ways to Buy Legumes:

■ dried - in bulk
■ dried - prepackaged
■ canned - ready to use

Where to Find Them:

■ Supermarkets   - in the bulk food department
                     - prepackaged, usually near the rice section
                     - canned with the other vegetables and in the specialty areas, e.g. Mexican

■ Bulk Food Stores - for dried only
■ Health Food Stores
■ Specialty Shops - e.g., Mexican, Italian, East Indian for canned and prepackaged

Special Notes:

■ Shop in a popular spot where you know the turnover is high. There is more assurance that your legumes will be fresh.
■ Avoid cracked, shrivelled beans. These are old and you will find them nearly impossible to soften even by long soaking and simmering.

Canned Beans & Lentils:

Have every variety on your shelf for jiffy meals as they are ready to use once they are rinsed and drained.

Beans We'd Like you to Know

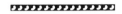

Betty Black Bean   The Split Peas   Lyle Lentil   Carlotta Chick Pea   Karl Kidney Bean

White Beans

- **Navy** - Small, white and oval, this bean is the most commonly known - your mother used them for baked beans.
- **Great Northern** - Same shape and colour as the navy bean but larger. Can be used interchangeably in any recipe calling for white beans, e.g. cannellini beans.
- **White Kidney** - Like the familiar red kidney only white. Can also be used interchangeably and substituted for cannellini beans.

Red Beans

- **Red Kidney** - Dark red/brown colour in the shape the name indicates. As well known as the navy bean, commonly used in chili.
- **Small Red or Mexican** - Called by these two names or a combination of both. Oval, smaller and darker red than the red kidney bean. Can substitute in any red bean recipe.
- **Pinto** - A lovely pinkish brown face with freckles. Smaller than the kidney beans, often used in Tex Mex cooking.

Black Beans

■ **Black or Turtle Beans** - Small, oval and glossy. Encourage your favourite shopping spot to stock them. Sometimes hard to find but worth the search.

And the Others

■ **Chick Peas or Garbanzo Beans** - A tan coloured, rough-skinned bean with an irregular round shape. Pleasant nutty flavour. Called by both names, but definitely a bean.

■ **Black-eyed Peas** - Cream coloured beans with an identity crisis. Mostly labelled "peas", but other times "beans". Recognizable by their black oval spot, mid-centre.

■ **Lima Beans** - In dried form, they are white and come in two sizes. Mealy texture. Frozen ones are green in colour and tasty. Also available canned.

Lentils and Split Peas

■ **Green/Brown** - Some stores label them brown, others green. We're fence sitting and calling them by both. They are small, flattened discs used in every area of legume cooking.

■ **Split Pea** - Both green and yellow, shaped exactly as you would expect – half a pea. Use mainly in soups.

Getting Started

xxxxxxxxxxxxxx

Beans and whole peas must be soaked.

Beans must be soaked before you cook them. Remember that chick peas (garbanzo beans) are really beans and must be treated as such. Lentils, split peas and black eyed peas do not require presoaking. There are two methods for soaking beans:

1) The Quick Soak Method:

- Sort through the beans, discarding the broken and shrivelled ones.
- Rinse beans under cold running water. A colander is useful for this step.
- Place beans in large saucepan and cover with three times the volume of water, e.g. for 1 cup/250 mL beans, use 3 cups/750 mL water.
- Bring to boil. Boil gently for 2-3 minutes. Remove from heat and let stand for at least one hour.
- Drain beans and rinse under cold running water again. Store in refrigerator or freezer.

2) The Slow Soak Method:

- As in the quick soak method, sort and wash beans.
- Place beans in a large bowl. Cover with 3 times as much fresh cold water as beans, e.g., 1 cup/250 mL beans to 3 cups/750 mL water.
- Let sit for at least 8 hours or overnight in a cool place.
- Drain water and rinse beans again. Refrigerate if not using immediately.

After soaking, you can do the following:

- For soups, stews, chilis or casseroles, use them directly as long as the recipe calls for at least 45 minutes cooking. The exception is chick peas (garbanzos) which need 1 hour 20 minutes.
- Cook them for salads and vegetables as outlined in the following cooking chart.
- Freeze for further use. Please label them "soaked". Two weeks later when you pull them out of the freezer, think they're cooked and toss them into a salad, your teeth will get a rude awakening.

Special Note:

- Lentils, split peas and black eyed peas don't need soaking but should be rinsed. Follow cooking chart directions.

Cooking Chart

Soaked Beans:	Cooking Time
Navy	35-40 min.
Great Northern	40-45 min.
Pinto	30-35 min.
Kidney, red or white	35-40 min.
Black	30-35 min.
Lima	55-60 min.
Chick Pea (Garbanzo)	1 hr 20 min.
Small Red	30-35 min.
Unsoaked Beans:	**Cooking Time**
Black-Eyed Peas	30 min.
Lentils & Split Peas	20-25 min.

Cooking Method:

- Place the soaked beans in a large saucepan. Cover with at least 3" (7.5 cm) of cold water.
- Bring to boil, reduce heat, cover and cook according to chart. Drain and rinse.
- Test for doneness by biting — try at least 5 beans. They should be tender but firm and have no taste of starchiness.

Special Notes:

If your beans aren't tender by the chart times, the reasons could be:

- Old beans. Try a more popular market.
- The altitude. The higher you are, the longer it takes.
- Hard water. Just keep cooking and "bite" testing. If they never soften, throw them out.

Yields:

Most Beans:

1 cup (250 mL) = 21/4 - 21/2 cups (550 - 625 mL) cooked.

Exceptions:

Chick peas (garbanzos), lima beans and Great Northern beans yield even more:

1 cup (250 mL) = 21/2 -3 cups (625 - 750 mL)

Canned Equivalents:

14 oz (398 mL) = 11/2 cups (375 mL)

19 oz (540 mL) = 21/4 cups (540 mL)

28 oz (796 mL) = 3 - 31/4 cups (750-796 mL)

The small yield differences are not of major importance. Bean recipes, especially in EASY BEANS, are flexible and forgiving.

Storing:

- Dried beans, peas and lentils should be kept in the cupboard in a moisture-proof lidded container. Try to use within the year.
- Soaked or cooked legumes stay fresh for a maximum of three days in the fridge. Store in a lidded container.
- Freeze in amounts that are reasonable for the recipes you use. Labelled ziploc bags and plastic cottage cheese containers, etc., are handy.

Cupboard Checklist

We have assumed your cupboard includes such herbs as basil, oregano and thyme, and spices such as chili powder and paprika. Listed below are some other ingredients that are special friends of a bean.

Dried Herbs and Spices

- **Bay Leaves** - A must. Add to beans while simmering. Remove before eating!
- **Coriander** - Comes ground or whole. Actually dried cilantro seeds but don't substitute for fresh cilantro – it has a very different taste.
- **Cumin (ground)** - Another must. A slightly bitter aromatic spice used in many Mexican and Middle Eastern recipes. Works well with chili powder.
- **Curry Powder** - A blend of spices common in Indian dishes. Buy a good brand, preferably East Indian.
- **Fine Herbs** - A combination of basil, thyme, rosemary, dill weed, savory, marjoram and parsley. Great when you can't decide what to use. Get 7 for the price of 1!
- **Italian Seasoning** - Another combination – oregano, basil, thyme, rosemary, sage and savory.
- **Garlic** - Fresh is best – but when in a hurry you can use garlic powder or processed minced garlic in jars.
- **Red Pepper Flakes** - Adds fire to any dish. Remember, a little goes a long way.
- **Savory** - Called the bean herb because it mates happily with all of them. Add to beans while simmering.
- **Turmeric** - An inexpensive substitute for saffron. It gives a pungent taste and a yellow colour to dishes.

Fresh Herbs

- Use fresh herbs if possible. Look for them in the specialty area of the vegetable department. In the summer you might even try growing your own. Fresh basil, oregano, thyme, dill weed and mint all add extra zip.
- **Cilantro** is available all year long at most supermarkets and is truly a bean herb. It has no substitute although fresh parsley is sometimes used. To keep cilantro fresh longer, stand its feet in water in a tall glass and put a plastic bag over the leaves. Secure with an elastic. Store in fridge.

Fresh Herbs to Dried is 3 to 1 e.g., 3 Tbsp (45 mL) fresh to 1 Tbsp (15 mL) dried.

You will also need:

- **Chilies** - We use small cans of diced green chilies for convenience. Often called for in Southwestern and Mexican recipes.
- **Dijon Mustard** - Our favourite, more expensive but definitely worth it.
- **Grains** - bulgar and couscous - Used in Middle Eastern recipes and available prepackaged in the specialty section of supermarkets. Also can be purchased in bulk.
- **Hot Pepper Sauce** - Tabasco sauce is the most common brand and can be used in place of jalapeno peppers.
- **Jalapeno Peppers** - buy fresh from the specialty area of vegetable departments. Watch out -- they are hot!
- **Olive Oil** - Choose a good quality extra virgin olive oil. Once again, it is more expensive but you'll taste the difference.
- **Salsa** - A spicy tomato dip or sauce, used to enliven some Mexican recipes.
- **Stock** - (vegetable, chicken or beef) - If you have time to make your own stock, great, but if not use good quality bouillon cubes or instant granules.
- **Vegetable Oil** - Safflower, sunflower or canola oils are the best.
- **Vinegars** - Balsamic, red wine, white wine, cider vinegars - all complement beans. They keep well, so stock up.

And Now for the Naughty Bits

Here are some suggestions that have been passed along to us in the year we have been researching beans and their sometimes embarrasing side effects:

- **Tolerance** - Build up tolerance by easing gently into the new world of bean cuisine. Start with only two recipes a week, perhaps trying the ones that don't have beans as their main ingredient (Cowboy Casserole, Minestrone Soup).

- **Preparation** - Discard the soaking water and rinse the beans. Then discard the cooking water and rinse in cold running water again.

- **Freezing** - Freeze the beans after the soaking stage. This hint has been given to us at parties, in bulk food stores and standing in supermarket lineups. No one can say why it works but it comes under the heading of "anything is worth a try if you have a problem."

- **Ginger** - Fresh or dried. Add a little of this spice to your bean dish and you'll never suffer again. This suggestion falls in the same category as Freezing.

- **Beano** - A liquid commercial product on sale in bulk food and drug stores. A few drops in the first forkful of your favourite dish and they guarantee you will never be socially unacceptable again.

STARTERS

Starters

Santa Fe Bean Salsa

*N*othing *seems to be more popular today than Mexican cuisine. Enjoy this wonderful variation on the classic salsa and try to stop yourself from shouting, Olé! Hopefully you have cooked black beans on hand for quicker preparation.*

2 cups	cooked black beans	500 mL
1	yellow pepper, chopped	1
1/2 cup	sweet white onion, chopped	125 mL
1	medium tomato, chopped	1
1	avocado, chopped*	1
1/2 cup	fresh cilantro, chopped	125 mL
3 Tbsp	olive oil	45 mL
	juice of one lemon	
2	cloves garlic, minced	2
1/8 tsp	red pepper flakes	0.5 mL

* Optional

- If using dried beans, soak and cook 3/4 cup (175 mL) of dried beans according to directions on pages 9 & 10. Rinse, drain and cool.
- Combine black beans, chopped pepper, onion, tomato, avocado and cilantro.
- In separate bowl, combine olive oil, lemon juice, garlic and pepper flakes. Pour over bean mixture.
- Stir and let stand for at least one hour.
- Serve with taco chips.

Makes 3 cups (750 mL)

Black Bean Quesadillas

*I*f you have leftover Mexican Baked Black Beans, recipe on page 86, this is a fast and easy appetizer or luncheon dish. You can be imaginative with your filling. One day when we ran out of the usual beans we used leftover Tuscany Lentil Salad and had a different taste treat.

1 1/2 cups	Baked Black Beans, recipe page 86	375 mL
8	medium size flour tortillas	8
3/4 cup	mozzarella or Monterey Jack cheese, grated	175 mL
1/2 cup	medium salsa	125 mL
1 Tbsp	olive oil	15 mL

- Spread 1/4 of the Baked Black Bean mixture onto 4 tortillas. Top each with 1/4 of the cheese and salsa.
- Place remaining 4 tortillas on top, pressing them down gently. Brush both sides lightly with oil. Arrange on a baking sheet.
- Bake for 5 minutes at 350ºF (180ºC) or until lightly browned and cheese is melted (can also be browned on the barbecue).
- Cut in eighths for appetizers, quarters for lunch.

Makes 16 appetizers or serves 4 for lunch.

Hot Bean Taco Dip

*A*s many times as this has been served, it always gets the same rave reviews. Nothing could be simpler to make!

16 oz	**light cream cheese**	**450 g**
8 oz	**light sour cream**	**225 g**
1 cup	**refried beans ***	**250 mL**
1	**pkg (1.5 oz/39 g) taco seasoning mix**	**1**
1 1/4 cups	**cheese ***	**300 mL**
	taco chips for dipping	

* Can use canned or recipe on page 106.

** Use a combination of cheddar and Monterey Jack.

■ Mix all the ingredients together, except the cheese and taco chips. Blend until smooth. Place in pottery casserole.

■ Grate cheese and spread on top of bean mixture.

■ Heat at 375°F (190°C) for 20-30 minutes until mixture is hot and the cheese is melted.

Serves 8-10.

Spicy Bean Vegetable Dip

*C*ompany is on their way over for a drink before an evening out. You
need an appetizer in a flash. This one takes only as long as rooting out
the blender or food processor and tossing everything in. If you have two
cups of red beans, make double -- there won't be any leftovers.

1 cup	canned kidney beans, drained and rinsed	250 mL
1	clove garlic, minced	1
1/4 tsp	hot pepper sauce (e.g. Tabasco)	1 mL
1 tsp	Worcestershire sauce	5 mL
1 Tbsp	mayonnaise	15 mL
	juice of 1/2 lemon	
1 tsp	minced chives or chopped green onions	5 mL
	raw vegetables for dipping	

- In food processor or blender, place all ingredients except chives. Blend until smooth.
- Put in serving bowl and sprinkle with chives.
- Serve with assorted raw vegetables (e.g. carrots, celery, peppers, broccoli, cauliflower, mushrooms).

Makes 1 cup (250 mL) of dip.

Bean Bonus

**Substitute any kind of canned or
cooked beans in the above recipe --
add chopped cilantro.**

Stuffed Mushroom Caps

▗▚▚▚▚▚▚▚▚▚▚▚▚▚▞▞

Y our guests will be guessing as they reach for their third and fourth. What exactly makes these mushroom morsels so yummy? Why, beans, of course. Much less expensive than the more traditional ham or shrimp filling. This mixture can be made the day before, stored in the fridge and the caps stuffed either in the morning or just before the party.

30	mushroom caps, stems removed	30
1	small onion, chopped	1
1	clove garlic, minced	1
	stems of 15 mushrooms, finely chopped	
1 Tbsp	olive oil	15 mL
1 tsp	ground cumin	5 mL
1 tsp	dried basil	5 mL
1/4 cup	fresh parsley, finely chopped	50 mL
	juice of 1 lemon	
1	can (19 oz/540 mL) chick peas	1
	(garbanzo beans), drained and rinsed	
1/2 cup	sesame seeds, toasted *	125 mL
3/4 cup	cheddar cheese (medium or sharp), grated	175 mL

* To toast sesame seeds, put on baking sheet and bake for 10 to 15 minute at 275ºF (140ºC). Watch them so they don't get too brown.

■ In skillet, sauté onion, garlic and mushroom stems in oil over medium heat until tender, about 5 minutes.

■ In food processor, combine all the ingredients except mushroom caps and cheese. Blend until smooth.

■ Stir in half the grated cheese. Stuff mushroom caps with bean and cheese mixture. Top with remaining cheese.

■ Place on baking sheet and bake for 10 minutes at 350ºF (180ºC). Serve hot.

Makes 30 appetizers.

Hummus

Y ou might have a yen for dipping those extra pita strips into a bowl of hummus -- but alas, no tahini in the fridge. Traditionally, sesame paste is a prime ingredient -- but this one is made without. Our secret is lots of lemon juice.

2	cloves garlic, minced	2
1	can (19 oz/540 mL) chick peas (garbanzo beans), drained and rinsed	1
6 Tbsp	fresh lemon juice	90 mL
2 Tbsp	olive oil	25 mL
1 tsp	ground cumin	5 mL
2 Tbsp	warm water	25 mL
3 drops	hot pepper sauce (e.g. Tabasco)	3
1 Tbsp	cilantro	15 mL

■ Combine all ingredients in a food processor or blender. Whirl until smooth.

■ Present in a glass or pottery bowl garnished with a cilantro sprig.

■ Serve with warm pita bread or raw vegetables.

Makes 2½ cups (625 mL)

Bean Bonus

Spread tortillas with Black Bean Hummus (opposite). Top with chopped tomatoes, diced onions and grated cheese. Pop in the oven for 10 min.

Black Bean Hummus

A 90's version of the traditional chick pea hummus but using the now trendy black bean. Handy as a base for the Bruschettas, page 22 or the Southern Pizza, page 88.

2 cups	cooked or canned black beans	500 mL
1/4 cup	tahini *	50 mL
2	cloves garlic, minced	2
1 tsp	ground cumin	5 mL
1/2 tsp	salt	3 mL
3 Tbsp	olive oil	45 mL
3 Tbsp	warm water	45 mL
	juice of one lime	
	juice of one lemon	

* Tahini is a sesame seed paste available in most food stores.

■ If you don't have cooked black beans on hand, soak and cook 3/4 cup (175 mL) dried black beans according to the directions on pages 9 and 10.

■ If using canned beans, drain and rinse.

■ Set aside a few whole beans for garnish.

■ Put all the ingredients in a food processor and blend until you have a smooth paste.

■ Place in small bowl. Garnish with parsley or cilantro and the few black beans you have saved.

■ Serve with warmed pita bread cut in bite-sized pieces.

Yields 2 1/2 cups (625 mL).

Black Bean Bruschettas

■■■■■■■■■■■■■■

*O*ur *version of this bite size Italian treat. For the base of these appetizers, you can use the black bean sauce from the Southern Pizza recipe, page 88, or the Black Bean Hummus on page 21. Both freeze well so don't be afraid to double the recipes.*

1	French baguette, cut in 1/2" (1 cm) slices	1
1 cup	Black Bean Sauce or Black Bean Hummus *	250 mL
1/2 cup	grated parmesan cheese	125 mL
Tomato Mixture:		
2	medium tomatoes, minced	2
1/2 cup	green onions, minced	125 mL
1 Tbsp	olive oil	15 mL
3 Tbsp	fresh basil, minced	45 mL
	freshly ground pepper	

* Black Bean Sauce, recipe page 88. Black Bean Hummus, see page 21.

■ Place baguette slices on a cookie sheet. Bake in 400ºF (200ºC) oven, turning once until lightly browned on both sides.

■ Spread Black Bean Sauce or Black Bean Hummus on slices.

■ Stir tomato mixture together and spoon onto slices. Top with parmesan cheese.

■ Place baguettes on cookie sheet. Bake in 400ºF (200ºC) oven for 4 minutes or until cheese starts to melt and topping is thoroughly heated.

Yields approximately 30.

More Bean Favourites

SOUPS

Soups

Classic Black Bean Soup

██████████████

*T*here seems as many variations of the traditional black bean soup as there are Elvis impersonators. This is the one we have found to be the most satisfactory. Cumin is a favoured spice but if it isn't one of yours, just eliminate it -- no problem.

2 cups	dried black beans	500 mL
1	meaty ham bone or ham hock	1
3 Tbsp	vegetable oil	45 mL
2	large onions, chopped	2
1	green pepper, chopped	1
4	cloves garlic, minced	4
10 cups	beef stock *	2.5 L
4	bay leaves	4
1/2 tsp	savory	3 mL
2 tsp	ground cumin	10 mL
1 tsp	dried oregano	5 mL
1/4 tsp	crushed red pepper	1 mL
1/2 cup	sherry	125 mL
	juice of 1/2 lemon	
	salt and pepper to taste	

* Can use bouillon cubes or instant beef granules. Follow package directions.

■ Soak beans by quick soak method on page 9. Rinse and drain.

■ In large soup pot, sauté onions, green pepper and garlic in oil over medium heat for 5 minutes.

■ Add beans, stock, ham bone, bay leaves and savory. Simmer 1 1/2 hours.

■ Remove bay leaves and ham hock. Take all the meat from the bone, dice and return to pot.

■ Take 4 cups (1 L) of beans and liquid and puree in a blender or food processor until smooth. Return mixture to soup pot.

■ Add cumin, oregano, crushed red pepper, sherry and lemon juice. Salt and pepper to taste. Stir well. Heat until piping hot.

Serves 8.

Puréed Black Bean Soup

Just as fast to prepare as the puréed white bean soup, as long as you have cans of black beans in the cupboard (or, of course, you soaked and cooked ones in the freezer). Fortunately, canned black beans can be found at Mexican stores and all supermarkets.

1	large onion, chopped	1
2	cloves garlic, minced	2
1 Tbsp	vegetable oil	15 mL
2 cups	chicken stock	500 mL
2	cans (14 oz/398 mL) black beans, rinsed	2
	and drained or 3 cups (750 mL) cooked beans	
1 tsp	cumin	5 mL
	sprigs of fresh cilantro or parsley – optional	

* Can use bouillon cubes or instant granules. Follow package directions.

■ If you are starting with dried beans, soak and cook 1 1/3 cups (325 mL) by the methods outlined on pages 9 and 10.

■ In a skillet, sauté onion, garlic in oil until brown and beginning to stick to the pan. Add 1/4 cup (50 mL) chicken stock and scrape browned bits free.

■ Pour into blender or food processor and add drained beans.

■ As the mixture whirls, slowly add the rest of the chicken stock and cumin. Pour into saucepan. Heat gently until simmering.

■ Serve in bowls topped with sprigs of parsley or cilantro.

Makes 4 small servings.

Tomato & Black Bean Soup

A very attractive looking soup with the combination of black beans, red tomatoes and white pasta. Tasty without the ingredients taking time to get to "know each other" as is the way with most soups. You could also call this Half Hour Soup because that's the length of time from first onion chopped to the table.

1	red onion, chopped	1
2	cloves garlic, minced	2
1 Tbsp	vegetable oil	15 mL
1	can (14 oz/398 mL) black beans, rinsed	1
	and drained or 1 1/2 cups cooked beans	
4 cups	chicken stock *	1 L
2	fresh tomatoes, chopped	2
1/2	red pepper, cut in thin short strips	1/2
1 cup	cooked macaroni	250 mL
1/2 tsp	freshly ground pepper	3 mL
1/2 cup	red wine	125 mL

* Chicken bouillon cubes or granules can be used. Follow package instructions.

■ If using dried beans, soak and cook 2/3 cup (150 mL) according to soaking and cooking instructions on page 9 and 10.

■ In soup pot, sauté onion and garlic in oil over medium heat for 5 minutes or until tender.

■ Add rest of ingredients and simmer gently for 15 minutes.

Serves 4.

Black & White Bean Soup

𝄢𝄢𝄢𝄢𝄢𝄢𝄢𝄢𝄢𝄢

*D*on't be frightened off by the long list of ingredients -- it is quickly assembled. The delicate sweet flavour of leeks and the tang of lime juice sets this soup apart from the its peers. Serve with Gramma's Corn Bread, page 111 in the Bread section.

1 cup	dried black beans	250 mL
1 cup	dried navy beans	250 mL
2 Tbsp	olive oil	25 mL
3	cloves garlic, minced	3
2	large leeks, chopped	2
4	medium carrots, chopped	4
1	medium onion, chopped	1
3	stalks celery, chopped	3
7 cups	beef stock *	1.75 L
2	bay leaves, crumbled	2
1/2 tsp	savory	3 mL
2 tsp	dried oregano	10 mL
1 tsp	dried thyme	5 mL
1/2 tsp	red pepper flakes (more if desired)	3 mL
1/4 cup	red wine (more if desired)	50 mL
	juice of one lime	
	salt and freshly ground pepper to taste	
1/2 cup	fresh parsley, chopped	125 mL

* Can use bouillon cubes or instant beef granules. Follow package directions.

- Soak beans by quick soak method, page 9. Drain and rinse.
- In soup pot, sauté garlic and vegetables in oil over medium heat for 5 minutes.
- Add beans, beef stock, bay leaves and savory. Bring to boil, reduce heat, cover and simmer for 1 hour or until beans are tender.
- Remove 3 cups (375 mL) of bean mixture and purée in blender or food processor until smooth. Stir back into soup.
- Add all other ingredients except parsley and simmer for another 10 minutes.
- Serve in bowls sprinkled with parsley.

Serves 6-8.

Picante Black Bean Soup

*W*e *love Black Bean Soup so much we've given you five recipes to choose from. Travel anywhere and you will discover that this type of soup is on most menus. Gourmet magazine calls black beans the trendy food of the 90s. We think they're as comforting as turning the electric blanket up to 9.*

1	large onion, chopped	1
3	cloves garlic, minced	3
5	strips bacon, cut in narrow pieces*	5
2	cans (14 oz/398 mL) black beans, drained and rinsed or 3 cups (750 mL) cooked beans	2
3 cups	chicken stock**	750 mL
1	red, green or yellow pepper, finely chopped	1
3/4 cup	salsa, medium strength	175 mL
1 1/2 tsp	ground cumin	8 ml

* Kitchen shears cut bacon easily.
** Can use bouillon cubes or instant granules. Follow package directions.

■ If you are starting with dried beans, soak and cook 11/3 cups (325 mL) by the methods outlined on pages 9 and 10.

■ In a large saucepan, sauté onion, garlic and bacon pieces for 5-8 minutes. Drain the fat.

■ Place 1 can or 1/2 the amount of cooked beans with 1 cup (250 mL) of chicken broth in a blender or food processor and whirl until smooth.

■ Add puréed mixture and remaining ingredients to saucepan. Simmer for 30 minutes over low heat.

Serves 4.

Leek & Lentil Soup

If your house/condo/apartment is on the market, this is the soup to have simmering on the stove. The wonderful aroma will convince potential buyers that this is the nest for them.

3 Tbsp	vegetable oil	45 mL
2	large leeks (white part plus 1/3 of the green, chopped)	2
1	medium onion, chopped	1
1	clove garlic, minced	1
1 cup	dried green/brown lentils	250 mL
1/4 cup	barley	50 mL
7 cups	chicken stock*	1.75 L
2	medium carrots, chopped	2
2	stalks celery, chopped	2
1	can (19 oz/540 mL) tomatoes, chopped	1
1	bay leaf, crumbled	1
1 tsp	dried thyme	5 mL
1 tsp	fine herbs	5 mL
1/4 cup	fresh parsley, chopped	50 mL
	salt and freshly ground pepper to taste	

* Can use 7 cups water and 2 large chicken bouillon cubes.

■ In soup pot, sauté leeks, onion and garlic in oil over medium heat until tender, about 5 minutes.

■ Wash and drain lentils. Add lentils, barley and chicken stock to soup pot. Bring to boil, reduce heat, cover and simmer for 45 minutes.

■ Add carrots, celery, tomatoes, bay leaf, herbs, salt and pepper and simmer for 30 minutes more or until vegetables are tender.

■ Add parsley and simmer another 5 minutes. Taste and adjust seasonings.

Serves 10.

Lebanese Lentil Soup

*T*his recipe has been prepared by all our family members for years. Gutsy and good as soon as it's made -- even better the next day. It also freezes well.

13/4 cup	green/brown lentils	425 mL
7 cups	water	1.75 L
4	beef bouillon cubes, crumbled	4
1	medium potato, chopped	1
2	bunches spinach, washed and coarsely chopped	2
2 Tbsp	vegetable oil	25 mL
1	onion, finely chopped	1
3	cloves garlic, minced	3
1 cup	fresh cilantro, chopped	250 mL
1/2 tsp.	ground pepper	3 mL
1 tsp	ground cumin	5 mL
3 Tbsp	lemon juice	45 mL

■ Rinse lentils. In soup pot, place lentils, water, bouillon cubes, potato and spinach. Bring to boil, reduce heat, cover and simmer for 45 minutes.

■ While lentils are cooking, heat oil in skillet and sauté onion and garlic over medium heat for 5 minutes.

■ Add onion mixture to lentils. Stir in cilantro, pepper, cumin and lemon juice. Simmer for 5 minutes more.

Serves 6-8.

Italian Lentil Soup

>>>>>>>>>>>>>>

Not all wonderful Italian restaurants are in Tuscany. We enjoyed a lentil soup in a superb restaurant in a Canadian provincial capital. Too shy to ask for the recipe, we created our own.

2 cups	dried green/brown lentils, rinsed	500 mL
12 cups	water	3 L
1	small ham hock *	1
2	zucchini, halved lengthwise and sliced	2
2	potatoes, halved lengthwise and sliced	2
2	onions, halved and sliced	2
6	carrots, sliced	6
4	stalks celery, sliced	4
1	can (28 oz/796 mL) crushed tomatoes	1
1 1/2 tsp	Italian seasoning **	8 mL
1 tsp	fine herbs ***	5 mL
1/2 tsp	salt	3 mL
	freshly ground pepper to taste	

* *4 beef bouillon cubes may be substituted for the ham hock.*

** *A blend of 6 herbs found in the spice section.*

*** *Another combination of herbs. See page 12.*

■ In soup pot, place lentils, water and ham hock. Bring to boil, reduce heat, cover and simmer for 2 hours.

■ Remove ham hock. Take meat off the bone and dice.

■ Add vegetables, tomatoes, herbs and diced meat to lentils. Simmer for 30 minutes more or until vegetables are tender.

■ Serve with freshly grated parmesan cheese. Freezes well.

Serves 10.

Lentil & Sausage Soup

*F*lexibility is the operative word with soup. We like this one spicy but if you don't, feel free to adjust the seasonings. However, the hot sausage is a must. Serve with Sesame Rounds, page 117 in the Bread section.

1	large onion, chopped	1
3	cloves garlic, minced	3
1/2 lb	spicy sausage, cut in 1/2" (1 cm) slices	225 g
1 Tbsp	vegetable oil	15 mL
10 cups	chicken stock *	2.5 L
2 cups	dried green/brown lentils, rinsed	500 mL
4	bay leaves	4
1 cup	carrots, sliced	250 mL
1 cup	celery, sliced	250 mL
1/2 cup	fresh parsley, chopped	125 mL
2 tsp	dried marjoram	10 mL
2 tsp	dried thyme	10 mL
	salt and pepper to taste	

* Can use bouillon cubes or instant granules. Follow package directions.

■ In large soup pot, heat oil and sauté onion, garlic and sausage over medium heat for 5 minutes. Drain fat.

■ Add chicken stock and lentils. Simmer covered for 30 minutes.

■ Add remaining ingredients. Simmer 25 minutes more. Remove bay leaves before serving.

Serves 8

Creamy White Bean Soup

The "not exotic anymore" *sun dried tomato is featured in this in-the-door and on-the-table soup. Perfect to take for work lunches in your thermos or a quick heat in the staff microwave. Use any cans of white beans you have in the cupboard. Large jars of sun dried tomatoes packed in oil are readily available and keep for weeks in the fridge.*

2	cans (19 oz/540 mL) navy beans	2
	or white kidney beans, drained and rinsed	
2 cups	chicken stock *	500 mL
5	sun dried tomatoes (packed in oil), chopped	5
2 tsp	oil (from tomatoes)	10 mL
6	green onions, chopped	6
1/2 cup	sherry	125 mL

* Can use bouillon cubes or instant granules.   Follow package instructions.

- ■ In food processor or blender, purée beans and broth.
- ■ In deep skillet, sauté green onions and tomatoes in oil over medium heat until onions are wilted but not brown.
- ■ Add sherry and stir until sherry is reduced by half. Remove from heat.
- ■ Add bean purée to skillet mixture, return to heat and gently stir for 3 min.
- ■ Pour into bowls and garnish with parsley or cilantro.

Serves 3-4.

Minestrone Soup

*A*nother version of an old favourite. Use your food processor to chop the vegetables to cut down on preparation time. Serve it as a hearty supper. Leftovers can be frozen in small containers for easy lunches.

1/2 cup	dried navy beans	125 mL
2 Tbsp	olive oil	25 mL
2	medium onions, chopped	2
2	cloves garlic, minced	2
10 cups	water	2.5 L
3	beef bouillon cubes, crumbled	3
3	carrots, chopped	3
2	potatoes, chopped	2
3	stalks celery, chopped	3
2	medium zucchini, chopped	2
1 cup	fresh or frozen green beans, chopped	250 mL
1	can (19 oz/540 mL) crushed tomatoes	1
2 Tbsp	fresh parsley, chopped	25 mL
1 tsp	fine herbs *	5 mL
1/2 tsp	dried oregano	3 mL
1/2 tsp	dried basil	3 mL
1/3 cup	macaroni **	75 mL
	freshly grated parmesan cheese	

* Fine herbs can be found in the spice section of grocery stores. See page 12.

** Macaroni doesn't freeze or reheat well, so only add it to the soup you're serving.

■ Soak beans using quick soak method on page 9. Drain and rinse.

■ In soup pot, sauté onions and garlic in oil over medium heat for 5 minutes.

■ Add beans, water and bouillon cubes. Bring to boil, reduce heat, cover and simmer for one hour.

■ Add vegetables, canned tomatoes and herbs. Simmer 1/2 hour more until vegetables are tender.

■ Add macaroni** and simmer for 10-15 minutes or until pasta is cooked.

■ Serve in bowls. Sprinkle with freshly grated parmesan cheese.

Serves 10-12

Seafood Minestrone

🙾🙾🙾🙾🙾🙾🙾🙾🙾🙾🙾🙾🙾

*U*se whatever white fish happens to be the most reasonably priced at the market. This is another speedy soup -- not the usual major chopping of vegetables as is called for in the classic minestrone. The broccoli gives it a fresh look but other vegetables, such as zucchini, thin skinned yellow squash or celery could be substituted.

2 cups	cooked navy, Great Northern or white kidney beans *	500 mL
1	large onion, chopped	1
2	cloves garlic, minced	2
1 Tbsp	vegetable oil	15 mL
4 cups	chicken stock **	1 L
1	can (28 oz/796 mL) tomatoes, chopped	1
1 cup	broccoli florets, cut small	250 mL
1 tsp	dried basil	5 mL
1/2 cup	salsa, medium strength	125 mL
1 cup	multicoloured pasta - your choice	250 mL
1 lb	white fish, cut in 1" (2.5 cm) pieces	450 g

* *Can substitute 1 can (19 oz/540 mL) of any white bean, drained and rinsed.*

** *Can use chicken bouillon cubes or instant granules. Follow package instructions.*

■ If using dried beans, soak and cook 3/4 of a cup (175 mL) according to instructions on page 9 and 10. Drain and rinse.

■ In large saucepan, sauté onion and garlic in oil over medium heat until tender – about 5 minutes.

■ Add remaining ingredients except fish. Bring to boil, reduce heat and simmer for 15 minutes.

■ Add fish and simmer 7 minutes longer.

Serves 6.

Beefy Bean Soup

*A*lthough this is speedy to prepare, like many soups its flavour improves as the ingredients get friendlier. A gutsy red wine enhances the taste and adds body. If you like cooking with wine and are dismayed by the ever increasing cost of a bottle, think about the "make it yourself clubs" and outlets. It's not time consuming and they've sprung up everywhere.

1 lb	ground beef	450 g
1	large onion, chopped	1
1	clove garlic, minced	1
1 Tbsp	vegetable oil	15 mL
1	small head of cabbage, coarsely chopped	1
1	can (14 oz/398 mL) crushed tomatoes	1
5 cups	water	1.25 L
1 cup	red wine	250 mL
1/4 tsp	crushed red pepper	1 mL
1 1/2 tsp	salt	7 mL
1 tsp	dried oregano	5 mL
1	can (19 oz/540 mL) white kidney beans, drained and rinsed	1
1/2 cup	freshly grated parmesan cheese	125 mL

■ In soup pot, cook beef, onions and garlic until beef is well browned.

■ With slotted spoon, remove beef mixture. To drippings add oil and cabbage. Cook over medium heat, stirring frequently until tender, about 8 to 10 minutes.

■ Add meat mixture, tomatoes, water, wine, crushed red pepper and salt. Bring to boil, reduce heat, cover and simmer for 30 minutes. Add more wine if desired.

■ Stir in beans, oregano and parmesan cheese. Heat through, about 10 minutes.

■ May serve with additional parmesan cheese sprinkled on top.

Serves 8.

Greek Bean Soup

*A Greek friend shared this traditional old country soup with us.
Although we have tasted similiar recipes, this one wins the blue ribbon.*

11/2 cups	dried navy beans	375 mL
9 cups	water	2.25 L
11/2 tsp	salt	7 mL
1/3 cup	olive oil	75 mL
1	large onion, chopped	1
2	cloves garlic, minced	2
4	medium carrots, chopped	4
3	stalks celery, chopped	3
1/2 cup	tomato paste	125 mL
1/2 tsp	freshly ground pepper	3 mL
1/2 tsp	dried oregano	3 mL
1/2 cup	fresh parsley, chopped	125 mL

- Soak beans using quick soak method on page 9. Drain and rinse.
- In soup pot, place beans, water and salt. Bring to boil, reduce heat, cover and simmer for 1 to 11/2 hours until beans are quite soft.
- While beans are cooking, heat oil in skillet and sauté vegetables over medium heat for 5 to 7 minutes.
- Add sautéed vegetables and tomato paste to beans. Simmer for 45 minutes more.
- Add more liquid if necessary. Add pepper, oregano and parsley and simmer for another 15 minutes. Adjust seasonings.

Serves 8.

Jiffy White Bean Soup

This soup is definitely in the category of "through the door and on the table". It makes a large pot of soup so the recipe can easily be halved (just cut the package of frozen spinach in half and keep in the freezer for another fast pot of soup).

1	large onion, chopped	1
2	cloves garlic, minced	2
2	stalks celery, chopped	2
2 Tbsp	vegetable oil	25 mL
6	medium carrots, chopped	6
7 cups	chicken stock *	1.75 L
1	pkg (10 oz/300 g) frozen chopped spinach	1
2	cans (19 oz/540 mL) white kidney beans, drained and rinsed	2
3 tsp	fine herbs **	15 mL
	salt and freshly ground pepper to taste	

* Can use chicken bouillon cubes or instant granules. Follow package directions.

** Fine herbs can be found in the spice section of grocery stores. See page 12.

■ In large saucepan, sauté onion, garlic and celery in oil over medium heat for 5 minutes.

■ Add stock and carrots. Cook until carrots are just tender. Add spinach and heat until defrosted.

■ Add beans, herbs, salt and pepper. Simmer 5 to 10 minutes more.

Serves 8.

Chicken Tortellini Soup

Italy meets the Orient and helps to solve the leftover chicken or turkey problem. Serve with crusty French bread.

1 cup	cooked white beans	250 mL
	(either navy or Great Northern)	
1/2 lb	cheese filled spinach tortellini	225 g
4 cups	water	1 L
2	chicken bouillon cubes *	2
2 Tbsp	white wine vinegar	25 mL
1 tsp	ground ginger	5 mL
2 Tbsp	soy sauce	25 mL
1 cup	cooked chicken (or turkey),	250 mL
	cut in small pieces	
2	bok choy stems and leaves, chopped	2
3	green onions, chopped	3

* Can use 2 tsp (10 mL) instant granules.

■ If starting with dried beans, soak and cook 1/2 cup (125 mL) according to directions on pages 9 and 10.

■ In medium saucepan, heat water, crumbled chicken cubes, vinegar, ginger and soy sauce to boiling. Add chicken, beans, onions and bok choy stems. Reserve leaves. Simmer 15 minutes.

■ While soup mixture is heating, cook tortellini as package directs. Drain and immediately add to simmering soup. Stir in bok choy leaves and simmer 3 more minutes.

Serves 4.

Spicy Tomato Soup

■■■■■■■■■■■■■■

This is as warm and soothing as a soup can be -- a real comfort food. For sick friends or relatives, it's the "chicken soup" of bean cuisine. Serve with Poppy Seed Fingers, page 113 in the Bread Section.

1/2 cup	dried navy beans	125 mL
2 Tbsp	vegetable oil	25 mL
1	large onion, chopped	1
2	cloves garlic, minced	2
2	stalks celery, thinly sliced	2
2	cans (28 oz/796 mL) whole tomatoes, chopped	2
2	cans (10 oz/284 mL) tomato soup	2
4 cups	water	1 L
1	large chicken bouillon cube or	1
	2 tsp (10 mL) chicken granules	
1 Tbsp	fresh parsley, chopped	15 mL
1 1/2 tsp	dried basil	7 mL
1 tsp	dried oregano	5 mL
1 tsp	dried thyme	5 mL
2 tsp	soy sauce	10 mL
	salt and freshly ground pepper to taste	

■ Soak beans using quick soak method on page 9. Drain and rinse.

■ In soup pot, sauté onion, garlic and celery in oil over medium heat until tender, about 5 minutes.

■ Add tomatoes, tomato soup, water, bouillon cube and navy beans. Bring to boil, reduce heat, cover and simmer for 1 hour.

■ Add parsley, herbs and soy sauce. Simmer 5 minutes more. Taste and adjust seasonings.

Serves 8.

Split Pea Soup

▪▪▪▪▪▪▪▪▪▪▪▪▪▪▪▪▪▪

*T*his has been a family favourite for many years. Makes a hearty supper and can be frozen in small containers for an easy lunch. Tasty accompaniment is Sesame Rounds, page 117 in the Bread section.

1	ham hock or leftover ham bone	1
12 cups	water	3 L
3 cups	dried split green peas, rinsed	750 mL
1	large onion, chopped	1
3	stalks celery, chopped	3
3	carrots, chopped	3
1 tsp	dried thyme	5 mL
1 tsp	dried oregano	5 mL
1/2 tsp	dried basil	3 mL
1 tsp	sugar	5 mL
	salt and pepper to taste	
1/2 cup	milk, optional	125 mL
	Croutons *	

* To make croutons, cut 6 slices of bread (preferably brown) into small cubes. Bake in oven at 250ºF (120ºC) for about 25 minutes or until lightly toasted.

■ In soup pot, combine all ingredients except milk. Bring to boil, reduce heat, cover and simmer for 2 hours.

■ Remove ham hock and take meat off bone. Dice meat.

■ If a smooth soup is desired, you may purée all of it in a blender or food processor.

■ Return diced ham to soup pot. Add milk just before serving. Adjust seasonings.

■ Serve in bowls sprinkled with croutons.

Serves 10.

Curried Pea Soup

*T*his is definitely a winner -- quick to prepare, only one hour to cook
and voilà, it is ready to serve! Be sure to use a good quality curry powder.

1 Tbsp	vegetable oil	15 mL
1	medium onion, chopped	1
1	clove garlic, minced	1
1 Tbsp	curry powder (more if desired)	15 mL
1 cup	dried split green peas, rinsed	250 mL
2	stalks celery, sliced	2
2	carrots, sliced	2
1	potato, peeled and diced	1
6 cups	chicken stock *	1.5 L
1	bay leaf	1
1 tsp	sugar	5 mL
	salt and pepper to taste	

* Can use chicken bouillon cubes or instant granules. Follow package directions.

■ In soup pot, sauté onion and garlic in oil over medium heat for 5 minutes.

■ Add remaining ingredients. Bring to boil, reduce heat, cover and simmer for one hour or until peas are soft.

■ Remove bay leaf and serve.

Serves 6.

Bean Bonus

**Reduce chicken stock and
use as a sauce over rice.**

Mulligatawny Soup

This classic eastern soup is not for the faint hearted. If you like curry, it's "to die for" as one of our favourite friends exclaimed. The lemon juice and soy sauce add an extra "bite".

1 cup	dried split yellow peas, rinsed	250 mL
1 Tbsp	olive oil	15 mL
1	medium onion, chopped	1
1	clove garlic, minced	1
1	medium carrot, chopped	1
2	stalks celery, chopped	2
2 tsp	curry powder (more if desired)	10 mL
1	bay leaf	1
6 cups	water	1.5 L
2	chicken bouillon cubes *	2
1/2 cup	cooked rice	125 mL
1	small apple, peeled and grated	1
1/4 tsp	dried thyme	1 mL
1 Tbsp	soy sauce	15 mL
1 Tbsp	lemon juice	15 mL
	freshly ground pepper	

* Can use instant granules. Follow package directions.

- In soup pot, sauté onion, garlic, carrot and celery in oil over medium heat for 5 minutes. Mix in curry powder and sauté for 3 minutes more, stirring frequently.
- Add bay leaf, water, bouillon cubes and split yellow peas. Bring to boil, reduce heat, cover and simmer for 45 minutes.
- Add rice, apple and thyme. Simmer for 15 minutes more. Remove bay leaf.
- Add lemon juice, soy sauce and pepper. Stir and serve.

Serves 6.

Two Bean Rotini Soup

*I*f you need a hearty inexpensive soup, this one will fill the bill. You can use either the large or small lima beans both of which are readily available packaged and in bulk. The beans you are looking for are white and not green as you might expect.

1 cup	dried lima beans	250 mL
1/2 cup	dried kidney beans	125 mL
6	strips bacon, cut in 1 " (2.5 cm) pieces	6
3	cloves garlic, minced	3
3	bay leaves	3
1 cup	celery, chopped	250 mL
1 cup	carrots, chopped	250 mL
1 cup	onions, chopped	250 mL
10 cups	water	2.5 L
2 Tbsp	chicken flavoured granules or	25 mL
	4 chicken bouillon cubes	
1 cup	uncooked rotini	250 mL
	salt and pepper to taste	

■ Prepare beans by quick soak method on page 9. Drain and rinse.

■ In large soup pot, sauté bacon, garlic and vegetables. If bacon does not produce enough fat, add a little oil.

■ Add presoaked beans and the rest of the ingredients except the rotini to the soup pot. Simmer covered for one hour adding more liquid if necessary. Stir occasionally.

■ Add rotini and simmer another 15 minutes, stirring often.

■ Before serving, remove bay leaves. Salt and pepper to taste.

Serves 6-8.

Moroccan Soup

*S*immering on the stove, this aromatic soup combines the exotic with the homey feeling always associated with soup "from scratch". Pita Triangles, page 116 in the Bread section are an ideal accompaniment.

1/2 cup	dried white beans (navy or Great Northern)	125 mL
2 Tbsp	vegetable oil	25 mL
2	medium onions, chopped	2
3	stalks celery, including leaves, chopped	3
1	can (19 oz/540 mL) tomatoes, chopped	1
3/4 cup	dried green/brown lentils	175 mL
8 cups	water	2 L
2 tsp	ground cinnamon	10 mL
1 1/2 tsp	ground ginger	7 mL
2 tsp	turmeric	10 mL
2	saffron threads, crumbled (optional)	2
2 Tbsp	fresh cilantro, finely chopped	25 mL
1/2 cup	fresh parsley, finely chopped	125 mL
	freshly ground pepper	
1	can (19 oz/540 mL) chick peas	1
	(garbanzo beans), drained and rinsed	
	juice of one lemon	
1/2 cup	fine vermicelli, broken in thirds	125 mL

- Soak white beans using quick soak method page 9. Drain and rinse.
- In soup pot, sauté onions and celery in oil over medium heat for 5 minutes. Add white beans, tomatoes, lentils and water. Bring to boil, cover, reduce heat and simmer for 1 to 1 1/2 hours.
- Add spices, cilantro, parsley, lemon juice and chick peas and simmer for another 15 minutes.
- Season to taste with salt and pepper. If you want the broth thickened, mash some of the beans against the side of the pot.
- At this point, the soup can be refrigerated or frozen (before vermicelli is added). If using immediately, add vermicelli and cook until tender, about 5 minutes.

Serves 8.

Quick Mediterranean Soup

*T*his soup earns the Good Housekeeping "double E" award - earthy and easy. It has a satisfying, lingering flavour of turmeric.

1	can (19 oz/540 mL) chick peas	1
	(garbanzo beans), drained and rinsed	
1/2 cup	fresh parsley, chopped	125 mL
1/4 tsp	freshly ground pepper	1 mL
1/2 tsp	turmeric	3 mL
1/2 tsp	ground ginger	3 mL
11/4 tsp	ground cumin	6 mL
1	small onion, grated	1
2	medium potatoes, peeled and diced	2
2 Tbsp	tomato paste	25 mL
6 cups	chicken stock *	1.5 L
8 drops	hot red pepper sauce (e.g. Tabasco)	8
1/4 cup	lemon juice	50 mL
1/4 cup	fresh cilantro, chopped	50 mL
	salt to taste	

* *Can use chicken bouillon cubes or instant granules. Follow package directions.*

■ In soup pot, place all ingredients except lemon juice and cilantro.
■ Simmer covered until potatoes and onions are cooked, about 30 minutes.
■ Add lemon juice and cilantro. Simmer 5 minutes more.
■ Adjust seasonings.

Serves 4.

Tomato, Garbanzo & Spinach Soup

*I*f *Popeye ever gave up his cans of spinach in favour of fresh, we're sure his favourite soup recipe would be this one. Olive Oyl could bring Dilly Crisps, page 117 in the Bread section.*

1	medium onion, chopped	1
2	cloves garlic, minced	2
1 Tbsp	vegetable oil	15 mL
2 cups	vegetable stock *	500 mL
2	cans (19 oz/540 mL) tomatoes,chopped	2
1	can (19 oz/540 mL) garbanzo beans	1
	(chick peas), drained and rinsed	
2 tsp	dried sage **	10 mL
3/4 cup	rotini	175 mL
2 cups	fresh spinach, chopped	500 mL
	salt and pepper to taste	

* *Can use a vegetable bouillon cube or chicken or beef stock if desired.*
** *6 fresh sage leaves if available.*

■ In large saucepan, sauté onion and garlic in oil over medium heat until tender - about 5 minutes.

■ Add stock, tomatoes, beans and sage. Simmer covered for 10 minutes.

■ Add rotini, simmer 10 minutes more. Add more stock if necessary.

■ Add spinach and simmer 5 more minutes. Adjust seasonings.

Serves 4-6.

Flexible Bean Soup

*T*hree Bean Soup -- 9 Bean Soup -- even 21 Bean Soup -- every number of bean soup mixtures is on sale from church bazaars to supermarkets. This is ours and its called "flexible" because you can use any combination of beans you have on your shelf. A good proportion is 2 to 21/2 cups of dried beans to 10 cups of vegetable or beef stock. The lentils and split peas are your thickening agents.

3/4 cup	each: dried white beans and pinto beans	175 mL
1/2 cup	each: dried kidney beans and chick peas	125 mL
2 Tbsp	vegetable oil	25 mL
2	medium onions, chopped	2
3	cloves garlic, minced	3
10 cups	beef or vegetable stock *	2.5 L
1/4 cup	each: dried yellow split peas,	50 mL
	green split peas and green/brown lentils	
2	bay leaves	2
1	can (14 oz/398 mL) crushed tomatoes	1
1/2	pkg (5 oz/150 g) frozen chopped spinach	1/2
11/2 Tbsp	fine herbs **	20 mL
	salt and freshly ground pepper to taste	

* *Bouillon cubes or instant granules can be used. Follow package instructions.*

** *Fine herbs can be found in the spice section of grocery stores. See page 12.*

■ Combine beans and soak using the quick soak method on page 9. Drain and rinse.

■ In soup pot, sauté onion and garlic in oil over medium heat for 5 minutes. Add beans and all other ingredients except tomatoes, spinach and fine herbs.

■ Reduce heat and simmer for 11/2 hours until beans are tender.

■ Add tomatoes, spinach and fine herbs. Simmer for 15 minutes more. Remove bay leaves.

■ If you wish to have a smoother soup, remove 4 cups of bean mixture and purée in food processor or blender. Return to pot.

Serves 8-10.

More Bean Favourites

More Bean Favourites

SALADS

Salads

Bean & Pasta Salad

🙟🙟🙟🙟🙟🙟🙟🙟🙟🙟🙟🙟

*T*his very colourful, large salad is perfect for luncheons or to take along on a group picnic. It is easy to assemble if you have cooked beans already prepared and waiting in your freezer (thaw before using, of course!). The French dressing used on this salad is excellent with any tossed salad so you may want to make extra and keep it in your fridge.

1 cup	cooked kidney beans*	250 mL
1 cup	cooked black beans*	250 mL
1 cup	cooked chick peas (garbanzo beans)*	250 mL
1 cup	cooked navy beans*	250 mL
2 cups	vegetable rotini, cooked **	500 mL
1	green pepper, chopped	1
1/2 cup	white onion, chopped	125 mL
1/4 cup	fresh parsley, chopped	50 mL
1 Tbsp	fresh basil (1 tsp/5 mL dried)	15 mL
1 Tbsp	fresh thyme (1 tsp/5 mL dried)	15 mL
French Dressing:		
2 Tbsp	white vinegar	25 mL
2 Tbsp	tomato ketsup	25 mL
1 Tbsp	brown sugar	15 mL
1/2 tsp	paprika	3 mL
2 tsp	lemon juice	10 mL
2 tsp	grated onion	10 mL
1/4 cup	oil (combination of half olive oil	50 mL
	and half vegetable oil works well)	

* *Use any combination of 4 cups leftover cooked or canned beans.*

** *If unavailable, use plain rotini.*

- ■ If using canned beans, drain and rinse.
- ■ In large salad bowl, combine beans, rotini, vegetables and herbs.
- ■ In tightly lidded jar, combine all dressing ingredients except oil. Blend well. Add oil and shake well.
- ■ Add dressing to bean mixture. Stir gently. Cover and refrigerate for several hours to meld flavours.

Serves 8-10.

Mixed Bean Salad

*W*hen it rains on your golf holiday and you're a bean nut, what would you do? Naturally, you're off to sample the local bean cuisine and southern California never lets you down. These delightful "mixed beans" were served in small bowls as an appetizer with warmed brown bread.

1 cup	fresh green beans, cut in 1/2" (1 cm) pieces	250 mL
1	can (19 oz/540mL) chick peas (garbanzo beans)	1
1	can (19 oz/540 mL) kidney beans	1
1	small sweet white onion, chopped	1
2 Tbsp	fresh parsley, chopped	25 mL
Lemon Dressing:		
1/4 cup	lemon juice	50 mL
3 Tbsp	olive oil	45 mL
2 tsp	Dijon mustard (grainy is nice)	10 mL
1 tsp	grated lemon rind (zest)	5 mL
1/2 tsp	freshly ground pepper	3 mL
1 tsp	sugar (optional)	5 mL

■ Steam green beans for about 5 minutes until crunchy but not soft.

■ Drain and rinse canned beans. Combine beans with onion and parsley.

■ In tightly lidded jar, combine dressing ingredients. Shake well.

■ Pour over salad and toss gently. Let stand for several hours for best flavour.

■ Serve on a bed of lettuce or spooned over a tossed salad.

Serves 4.

Black Bean Tomato Salad

*W*ith *the availability of fresh herbs in the supermarket, this salad can be enjoyed all year round. Another one that can be prepared very quickly using leftover or canned beans. This recipe is very eye-appealing served in a glass salad bowl.*

4	ripe tomatoes, cut in chunks	4
11/4 cups	feta cheese, cut in chunks, half the size of the tomatoes	300 mL
1/3 cup	black beans, cooked or canned	75 mL
1/4 cup	fresh basil	50 mL
Dressing:		
3 Tbsp	olive oil	45 mL
2	cloves garlic, minced	2
1/2 tsp	sugar	3 mL
1/4 tsp	pepper	1 mL

■ Prepare first four ingredients and place in salad bowl. Stir gently to mix.

■ In tightly lidded jar, combine dressing ingredients. Shake well. Pour over salad mixture and toss lightly.

■ Let stand for one hour in the refrigerator. Keeps for three days if tomatoes are firm.

Serves 4.

Black Bean & Rice Salad

This tangy salad is very colourful with its yellow corn, black beans and red pepper pieces. We suggest you don't use canned beans -- they can be a little soft and not as black as the ones cooked from scratch.

3/4 cup	dried black beans	175 mL
1 cup	cooked long grain rice	250 mL
1/2 cup	kernel corn, canned or fresh	125 mL
1	sweet red pepper, chopped	1
3	green onions, chopped	3
2 Tbsp	fresh cilantro, chopped	25 mL
2 Tbsp	fresh parsley, chopped	25 mL
Dressing:		
1/4 cup	olive oil	50 mL
2 Tbsp	red wine vinegar	25 mL
1 Tbsp	lemon juice	15 mL
1 1/2 tsp	chili powder (or to taste)	8 mL
1	clove garlic, minced	1
1/2 tsp	ground cumin (or to taste)	3 mL
	salt and pepper to taste	

■ Quick soak and cook beans according to instructions on pages 9 and 10 (be sure not to overcook – you want them just tender but not mushy). Rinse and cool.

■ In salad bowl, combine all ingredients except dressing.

■ In tightly lidded jar, combine dressing ingredients. Shake well.

■ Pour over salad and toss gently.

■ Refrigerate for several hours before serving. Still good three days later.

Serves 6.

Southwestern Potato Salad

If you have been making the same traditional potato salad for more years than you would care to admit, try this one. We guarantee instant approval and widespread demand for copies of this recipe! It also uses up those cooked black beans hiding in the freezer.

6	large red or white, thin skinned potatoes	6
1/2 lb	bacon	225 g
1	can (4 oz/114 mL) diced green chilies, drained 1	
1/2 cup	cooked black beans	125 mL
1/2 cup	fresh parsley, chopped	125 mL
1/2 cup	red onion, chopped	125 mL
Dressing:		
3 Tbsp	vegetable oil	45 mL
1/3 cup	white wine vinegar	75 mL
1/2 tsp	salt	3 mL
1/4 tsp	pepper	1 mL
1/2 tsp	ground cumin	3 mL

- Cook unpeeled potatoes in covered saucepan for 20 minutes or until just tender. Drain and let cool.
- Cook bacon in skillet until crisp. Remove, pat dry and crumble.
- In large salad bowl, cube unskinned potatoes. Add remaining ingredients.
- In tightly lidded jar, combine dressing ingredients. Shake well. Pour over salad mixture and toss lightly.
- Cover and refrigerate for at least two hours so that the ingredients get to know each other.

Serves 6.

Layered Bean Slaw

▟▟▟▟▟▟▟▟▟▟▟▟▟▟▟

*T*his recipe can be expanded or contracted depending on the number of people you are feeding. Be experimental with the layers but be sure to show it off in a glass bowl. Why not play the role of maestro and toss it at the table!

1	red onion, cut in rings and halved	1
2 cups	shredded green cabbage	500 mL
2	tomatoes, sliced and halved	2
1	small cucumber, thinly sliced	1
1	pepper, yellow, green or red	1
1	can (14 oz/398 mL) black beans, drained and rinsed or 1 1/2 cups cooked*	1
3/4 cup	feta cheese, crumbled	175 mL
Dressing:		
1/2 cup	vegetable oil	125 mL
1/3 cup	red wine vinegar	75 mL
2	cloves garlic, minced	2
1/2 tsp	ground cumin	3 mL
	salt and pepper to taste	

* If using dried beans, soak and cook 3/4 cup (175 mL) according to directions on pages 9 and 10.

■ In glass bowl, layer ingredients in the order listed, starting with the onion on the bottom and finishing with a top layer of feta cheese. Cover and refridgerate.

■ In tightly lidded jar, combine dressing ingredients. Shake well.

■ When ready to serve salad, pour on dressing and take to the table. Toss in front of family or guests.

Serves 6

Checkerboard Bean Salad

*L*ike all great women this dish improves with age, so for the best flavour, make it at least 8 hours in advance. The checkerboard effect comes from using both black and white beans.

1/2 cup	dried black beans *	125 mL
1/2 cup	dried navy beans *	125 mL
1/4 cup	sweet white onion, chopped	50 mL
1/2 cup	red bell pepper, chopped	125 mL
1/2 cup	kernel corn, canned or fresh	125 mL
1/4 cup	fresh cilantro, chopped	50 mL
Dressing:		
1/4 cup	olive oil	50 mL
2 Tbsp	cider vinegar	25 mL
1 tsp	cumin	5 mL
1/2 tsp	dry mustard	3 mL
1 tsp	sugar	5 mL
1	clove garlic, minced	1
	freshly ground pepper to taste	

* This salad is quickly made if you have cooked beans on hand.

■ Soak and cook black and navy beans separately, following directions on pages 9 and 10. Don't overcook.

■ Drain and rinse with cold water.

■ In a large bowl, combine beans, vegetables and cilantro.

■ In tightly lidded jar, combine dressing ingredients.   Shake well. Add to bean mixture. Toss lightly.

Serves 4.

Couscous & Chick Pea Salad

*T*his *salad really needs fresh mint to make it perfect. In the summer, there's lots but in the winter it is always a major search in the produce department. Sometimes it's available, sometimes not. Leftovers will last in the fridge for 3-4 days.*

13/4 cups	water	425 mL
1 cup	couscous	250 mL
1	can (14 oz/396 mL) chick peas (garbanzo beans), drained and rinsed	1
2	small red peppers, chopped	2
4	green onions, thinly sliced	4
2	medium carrots, finely chopped	2
1/2 cup	pitted Greek olives, diced	125 mL
6 oz.	feta cheese, crumbled	170 g
Dressing:		
6 Tbsp	fresh mint	90 mL
1 1/2 Tbsp	white wine vinegar	20 mL
1	clove garlic, minced	1
1/2 tsp	Dijon mustard	3 mL
1/4 tsp	sugar	1 mL
1/3 cup	olive oil	75 mL

- In medium saucepan, bring water to the boil. Add couscous.
- Remove from heat, cover and let stand for 5 minutes.
- In large bowl place couscous and fluff with a fork. Add all other salad ingredients except feta cheese.
- In food processor or blender, add all dressing ingredients except oil. Process a few seconds until mint is finely chopped. Gradually add oil and process until well blended.
- Pour dressing over salad. Toss. Add feta cheese and stir gently.
- Arrange lettuce around edge of large platter or glass salad bowl. Mound salad in the centre.

Serves 6-8.

Garbanzo & Black Olive Salad

*I*f you like black olives you've found your salad. Line a salad bowl with lettuce leaves and serve with Dilly Crisps, page 117 in the Bread Section.

2	cans (19 oz/540 mL) chick peas	2
	(garbanzo beans), drained and rinsed	
2	large stalks celery, chopped	2
2	green peppers, chopped	2
1/2 cup	red onion, chopped	125 mL
1/4 cup	fresh parsley, chopped	50 mL
1 cup	pitted ripe black olives, cut in quarters	250 mL
Dressing:		
1	pkg (3/4 oz/ 21 g) Italian Salad Mix	1

- In salad bowl, combine salad ingredients.
- In tightly lidded jar, prepare salad dressing following package instructions. Use red wine vinegar.
- Combine dressing and salad ingredients. Toss lightly.
- Chill. Keeps well in fridge for 3 days.

Serves 8.

Bean Bonus

Try using pesto sauce as the dressing in the above recipe or any of the mixed bean salads.

Garbanzo Potato Salad

▸▸▸▸▸▸▸▸▸▸▸▸▸▸▸▸

*E*asy *to expand for a crowd. Also another good keeper. If your potatoes are mealy (sometimes its hard to tell when your're buying them) they tend to absorb the dressing all too readily. If the salad seems dry, mix up some more dressing and add.*

3 cups	cooked, peeled and cubed potatoes	750 mL
1 cup	uncooked carrots, sliced thinly	250 mL
1	red onion, sliced thinly	1
1 cup	canned garbanzo beans (chick peas),	250 mL
	drained and rinsed	
Dressing:		
1/2 cup	wine vinegar	125 mL
1/4 cup	vegetable oil	50 mL
1/2 tsp	sugar	3 mL
2	cloves garlic, minced	2
	salt and pepper to taste	

■ Steam carrots until just tender – 4 minutes.

■ Place all the salad ingredients together in a large bowl.

■ In a tighlty lidded jar combine dressing ingredients. Shake well.

■ Pour dressing over salad and stir well.

■ Chill in fridge for 2 hours.

Serves 4-6

Tabouli

*T*astiest when fresh mint is available. During the winter, dried mint is acceptable or you can leave the mint out altogether. Bulgar wheat is now universally available in bulk or prepackaged at your local grocery store. The amounts of the vegetables can be varied without detriment to the flavour -- we lean towards lots of parsley.

1 1/2 cups	bulgar wheat (cracked wheat)	375 mL
1	can (19 oz/540 mL) chick peas	1
	(garbanzo beans), drained and rinsed	
1 1/2 cups	fresh parsley, chopped	375 mL
3/4 cup	fresh mint, chopped	175 mL
3/4 cup	green onions, chopped	175 mL
3/4 cup	tomatoes, cut into small pieces	175 mL
Dressing:		
1/4 cup	vegetable oil	50 mL
1/2 cup	lemon juice	125 mL
	salt and pepper to taste	

■ Place bulgar wheat in a bowl and pour boiling water to cover by at least one inch. Let stand for 1/2 hour until all the water has been absorbed. Drain any excess and pat dry with a paper towel if necessary.

■ Stir in remaining ingredients except dressing.

■ In small bowl, whisk oil, lemon juice and salt and pepper. Pour over salad and mix well.

■ Chill in fridge for at least one hour. This salad, covered and cold, will keep for up to four days.

Serves 8.

Feta Garbanzo Salad

*S*hades of the Greek Isles - easy to whip up at the summer cottage for a simple family or party dinner. Serve with sliced meats and try the Dilly Crisps in the Bread section, page 117.

1	can (19 oz/540 mL) garbanzo beans	1
	(chick peas), drained and rinsed	
1/2 cup	black olives, sliced	125 mL
1	red onion, chopped	1
1/2 cup	feta cheese, crumbled	125 mL
1/2 cup	fresh parsley, chopped	125 mL
Dressing:		
1/2 cup	vegetable oil	125 mL
1/4 cup	lemon juice	50 mL
1/4 tsp	black pepper	1 mL
1/2 tsp	dried oregano	2 mL
1 tsp	Dijon mustard	5 mL

- In medium bowl, mix garbanzo beans, olives, onions, cheese and parsley.
- In tightly lidded jar, combine dressing ingredients. Shake well.
- Pour dressing on salad mixture. Stir.
- Chill in refrigerator for one hour.
- Serve in a lettuce lined glass or pottery dish.

Serves 4.

Bean Bonus

To add zest to a tossed salad, spoon any leftover bean salad over lettuce or spinach.

Texas Chicken Salad

A dinner staple for lazy summer days. Leftover roasted or barbecued chicken can be used as well as starting from scratch. Best of all, it can be eaten with a napkin tucked under your chin, lounging in a deck chair.

2	chicken breasts, skinned and cubed	2
2 Tbsp	vegetable oil	25 mL
1/2 cup	salsa, medium strength	125 mL
1/2 cup	light salad dressing or mayonnaise *	125 mL
1/2 tsp	hot pepper sauce (e.g. Tabasco)	3 mL
1	avocado, chopped	1
2	medium tomatoes, chopped	2
3 cups	shredded lettuce	750 mL
3 cups	tortilla chips	750 mL
1	can (19 oz/540 mL) red kidney beans, drained and rinsed	1
1/2 cup	Monterey Jack cheese, grated	125 mL

* Can use regular salad dressing.

- In skillet, heat oil and stir-fry chicken for 5 minutes or until pink disappears. Stir in salsa and simmer for 5 more minutes.

- Place tomatoes and avocados in a bowl. Add combined salad dressing and hot pepper sauce. Stir gently.

- On large serving plate or individual plates, layer in the following order. Start with chips, then lettuce, beans, chicken and ending with tomato and avocado mixture. Top with cheese.

Serves 6.

Taco Salad

ΣΣΣΣΣΣΣΣΣΣΣΣΣΣ

*T*his is a "complete meal" salad to serve on a hot summer night or when you are having guests for lunch. Everything can be prepared ahead and tossed together at the last moment.

1	large onion, chopped	1
1	clove garlic, minced	1
1 Tbsp	vegetable oil	15 mL
1/2 lb	lean ground beef	225 g
1	can (71/2 oz/213 mL) tomato sauce	1
1 tsp	chili powder (more if desired)	5 mL
1 tsp each	ground cumin, dried oregano	5 mL
	freshly ground pepper to taste	
1	large iceberg or leaf lettuce	1
2	large tomatoes, chopped	2
1	can (14 oz/398 mL) kidney beans,	1
	drained and rinsed	
1/2 cup	black olives, sliced (optional)	125 mL
1	avocado, chopped (optional)	1
2 cups	taco or corn chips	500 mL
1/2 cup	grated cheddar or Monterey Jack cheese	125 mL
Dressing:		
1/3 cup	vegetable oil	75 mL
3 Tbsp	wine vinegar	45 mL
1/4 tsp each	salt, sugar, dry mustard	1 mL

■ In skillet, sauté onion and garlic in oil over medium heat for about 5 minutes. Add beef and brown. Drain excess fat.

■ Add tomato sauce, spices and oregano. Simmer for 10 minutes. Cool.

■ Cut lettuce in bite sized pieces and place in large salad bowl.

■ Combine meat mixture, tomatoes, kidney beans, olives, avocado and 1/2 the taco chips. Add to lettuce.

■ In tightly lidded jar, combine dressing ingredients. Shake well.

■ Combine dressing with salad ingredients. Mix gently. Top with other half of the taco chips and cheese.

Serves 6–8.

Kidney Bean & Feta Salad

****

*W*hen preparing a stress-free dinner party, the secret is to find easy-to-make recipes that taste like you slaved for hours. Here is one of our treasures. Guests will also appreciate the Herb Bread, on page 116 in the Bread Section.

1	can (19 oz/540 mL) red kidney beans	1
2 cups	cabbage, finely chopped	500 mL
1	red pepper, chopped	1
2	green onions, chopped	2
1/2 cup	feta cheese, cubed	125 mL
3 Tbsp	fresh parsley, chopped	45 mL
Dressing:		
2 Tbsp	lemon juice	25 mL
1 Tbsp	vegetable oil	15 mL
1	clove garlic, minced	1
1/2 tsp	dried basil, optional	3 mL

■ Drain and rinse kidney beans.

■ In salad bowl, combine beans, vegetables, feta cheese and parsley.

■ In tightly lidded jar, combine dressing ingredients and shake well.

■ Combine dressing with salad ingredients. Toss lightly.

■ Cover and refrigerate until chilled.

Serves 4.

Nutty Lentil Salad

*F*rom humble to fashionable in 5 years. That's the story of the lentil in the 90's. Innovative chefs -- at home or in leading edge restaurants -- appreciate their rich and earthy versatility.

11/2 cups	dried green/brown lentils, rinsed	375 mL
2	red apples, skins on and chopped	2
1	stalk celery, chopped	1
3/4 cup	pecans, chopped	175 mL
2 Tbsp	parsley, finely chopped	25 mL
Dressing:		
1/3 cup	vegetable oil	75 mL
2 tsp	Dijon mustard	10 mL
2 Tbsp	cider vinegar	25 mL
1/2 tsp	salt	2 mL

- In large saucepan, place lentils in 6 cups (1.5 L) water. Bring to boil, reduce heat, cover and simmer for 20 to 25 minutes until barely tender. Do not overcook. Drain and rinse in cold water
- In tightly lidded jar, combine dressing ingredients. Shake well.
- In salad bowl add dressing to lentils. Toss well. Add other salad ingredients and mix. Chill in fridge for at least one hour before serving.

Serves 6-8.

Tuscany Lentil Salad

*B*alsamic vinegar makes almost anything taste superb. It is especially delicious in dishes such as this lentil salad which conjures up the great flavours of Italy.

1 cup	dried green/brown lentils	250 mL
3 cups	water	750 mL
1	bay leaf	1
1/2 cup	white onion, finely chopped	125 mL
1/4 cup	green pepper, chopped	50 mL
1/2 cup	red pepper, chopped	125 mL
1/2 cup	carrots, coarsely chopped	125 mL
Dressing:		
2 Tbsp	olive oil	25 mL
3 Tbsp	balsamic vinegar	45 mL
1 tsp	sugar	5 mL
1/2 tsp	dry mustard	3 mL
1 tsp	dried basil (or 1 Tbsp/15 mL fresh)	5 mL
1	clove garlic, minced	1

■ Rinse lentils. Place in saucepan with water and bay leaf. Cover and simmer for about 20 to 25 minutes until lentils are just tender (do not overcook or they will become mushy).

■ Drain and rinse lentils. Discard bay leaf. Cool.

■ In a large bowl, combine lentils with vegetables.

■ In a tightly lidded jar, combine dressing ingredients. Shake well.

■ Combine dressing with other ingredients and mix gently.

■ Chill several hours (it is inclined to get soggy if left overnight). Serve on a bed of lettuce or spooned over a tossed salad.

Serves 6.

Orange White Bean Salad

████████████████

*T*his salad is so refreshing and eye appealing it's a pity we've had to give up serving it. All who tried it -- and there were many -- enjoyed it so much we had to share the recipe -- and now they're sharing with their friends! Hopefully it will be a find for you. Keeps for three days covered in the fridge.

21/2 cups	cooked navy, white kidney or	625 mL
	Great Northern beans *	
1	large orange, peeled and diced,	1
1	green pepper, chopped	1
4	green onions, sliced including green parts	4
1/2 cup	fresh parsley, chopped	125 mL
Dressing:		
1/4 cup	vegetable oil	50 mL
3 Tbsp	white wine vinegar	45 mL
1 tsp	sugar	5 mL
1/2 tsp	Dijon mustard	3 mL

* *You can substitute 19 oz/540 mL of canned beans, drained and rinsed.*

■ Prepare 1 cup dried beans by quick soak method on page 9. Cook according to chart on page 10. Be sure you don't overcook the beans. You want them tender but not mushy so give them the "bite" test after 35 minutes.

■ Drain, rinse and cool beans. Place in bowl and add the rest of the ingredients.

■ In tightly lidded jar, combine dressing ingredients. Shake well. Add to bean mixture and stir gently.

■ Chill in fridge for at least one hour.

■ Serve in lettuce lined individual bowls, garnished with unpeeled orange slice twists.

Serves 6.

Xmas Bean Salad

So named for obvious colour reasons. However, it's too tasty to only serve during the festive season. Think about it in January when the Visa bill arrives -- the salad works out to be pennies per serving.

3 cups	cooked navy or Great Northern beans *	750 mL
1	red pepper, chopped	1
1	green pepper, chopped	1
3	green onions, sliced (include green parts)	3
Dressing:		
1/2 cup	orange juice	125 mL
1/3 cup	balsamic vinegar	75 mL
1 Tbsp	dried basil or 1/4 cup (50 mL) fresh, chopped	15 mL
	salt and pepper to taste	

* Substituion: 2 cans (14 oz/398 mL) white beans, drained and rinsed.

- Soak and cook 11/3 cups (325 mL) beans as outlined on pages 9 and 10. Be sure to give the beans the "bite test" after 35 minutes. They should be tender but not mushy.
- Cool beans. In bowl combine beans, peppers and onions.
- In tightly lidded jar, combine dressing ingredients. Shake well.
- Add dressing to bean mixture. Stir.
- Chill in fridge for at least 2 hours.
- Serve in lettuce lined salad bowl. You can also heap the bean mixture on thickly sliced tomatoes if you want individual portions.

Serves 6.

More Bean Favourites

,,,,,,,,,,,,,,,,

More Bean Favourites

Main Dishes

Vegetarian Chili

** JJJJJJJJJJJJJJJJJ**

*T*he secret to the fresh taste of this chili is the lemon juice and not overcooking it. If you don't have a meatless chili in your repertoire, this is the one. Adjust the seasonings to your taste.

3 Tbsp	vegetable oil	45 mL
2	large white onions, chopped	2
3	cloves garlic, minced	3
2	green peppers, chopped	2
1	can (28 oz/796 mL) tomatoes, chopped	1
4	small zucchini, sliced 1/4" (1 cm) thick	4
2	cans (19 oz/540 mL) chick peas (garbanzo beans), drained and rinsed	2
2	cans (19 oz/540 mL) kidney beans, drained and rinsed	2
1 Tbsp	chili powder	15 mL
1 Tbsp	ground cumin	15 mL
1 Tbsp	dried basil	15 mL
1 Tbsp	dried oregano	15 mL
1 tsp	salt	5 mL
1 tsp	pepper	5 mL
1/2 cup	fresh parsley, chopped	125 mL
1/4 cup	lemon juice (fresh if possible)	50 mL

■ In skillet, sauté onions, peppers and garlic in oil over medium heat for 5 minutes.

■ Transfer to large, top-of-the-stove pot and add tomatoes and zucchiini. Cook, uncovered, for 30 minutes.

■ Stir in chick peas, kidney beans, spices, herbs, parsley and lemon juice. Cook for 15 minutes more.

■ Serve in large bowls with your choice of accompaniment from the Bread section.

Serves 6–8.

Champion Black Bean Chili

*S*o called because after losing the first game of an 8-team summer cottage volleyball tournament, our group tucked into heaping bowls of this chili. To the chant of "bean power" from our supporters, the team didn't lose another game and the championship was ours.

2 cups	dried black beans	500 mL
6 cups	water	1.5 L
4	bay leaves	4
3	cloves garlic, minced	3
2	large onions, chopped	2
3 Tbsp	vegetable oil	45 mL
1	can (28 oz/796 mL) tomatoes, undrained	1
2	fresh jalapeno peppers, minced	2
2 Tbsp	chili powder (more if desired)	25 mL
1 tsp	salt	5 mL
2 tsp	ground cumin (more if desired)	10 mL
1 Tbsp	dried oregano	15 ml
1 cup	red wine	250 mL
1/2 cup	fresh cilantro or parsley, chopped	125 mL

■ Prepare dried beans by quick soak method on page 9. Discard soaking water, rinse beans and add 6 cups of fresh water plus bay leaves. In large pot, simmer, covered, for 30 minutes.

■ While the beans are cooking, in skillet sauté onions and garlic in oil over medium heat. Add tomatoes, breaking them up as you stir. Add peppers, spices and oregano. Simmer 10 minutes.

■ When beans are cooked, remove 2 cups (500 mL) of bean liquid and reserve. Add skillet mixture to beans. Simmer 25 minutes. The mixture should be "loose but not runny". Use the reserved bean liquid when necessary.

■ Add wine and cilantro and continue to simmer another 10 minutes. Taste, adjust seasonings if necessary.

■ Serve in individual bowls accompanied by slices of thick French bread.

Serves 6-8.

Seafood Chili

The beauty of this simple recipe is you can use any white fish. Our suggestions are sole, cod, red snapper, halibut, turbot or any light fleshed fish you are presented with by your fishing friends.

1 lb	white fish of your choice	450 g
3 Tbsp	vegetable oil	45 mL
2	large onions, chopped	2
1	green pepper, chopped	1
1	yellow pepper, chopped	1
1 cup	celery, chopped	250 mL
2	cloves garlic , minced	2
1	can (28 oz/796 mL) tomatoes, chopped	1
1	can (19 oz/540 mL) kidney beans, drained and rinsed	1
1/2 cup	fresh parsley, chopped	125 mL
1 tsp	chili powder (more if desired)	5 mL
	salt and pepper to taste	

■ In large skillet, sauté onions, peppers, celery and garlic in oil over medium heat for 5 minutes.

■ Transfer into large pot and add the remaining ingredients except the fish. Cover and simmer for 30 minutes.

■ Cut fish into 1" (2.5 cm) pieces and add to pot. Simmer for another 15 minutes.

Serves 4.

Snow Chili

A quiet, unobtrusive dish, this chili is not an immediate attention grabber. However, it is surprisingly tasty. Dress it up with fresh cilantro and serve it with Gramma's Corn Bread, page 111 in the Bread section.

1	large onion, chopped	1
3	cloves garlic, minced	3
3 Tbsp	vegetable oil	45 mL
2 cups	cooked chicken or turkey (more if desired)	500 mL
3 cups	chicken stock *	750 mL
2	cans (19 oz/540 mL) Great Northern beans, navy or white kidney beans **	2
1 tsp	ground red chilies	5 mL
1/4 tsp	ground cloves, optional	1 mL
1 Tbsp	dried basil	15 mL
1/4 cup	fresh cilantro, chopped	50 mL

* Can use bouillon cubes or instant granules. Follow package directions.

** If using dried beans, soak and cook 2 cups according to pages 9 & 10.

■ In large saucepan, sauté onion and garlic in oil over medium heat until tender but not brown.

■ Add rest of ingredients except cilantro and simmer 40 minutes, stirring occasionally. If chili becomes too thick or dry during cooking, add more chicken stock.

■ About 5 minutes before serving, add cilantro.

Serves 6.

Black-eyed Pea Chili

*C*onfusion reigns among recipe writers, bean producers, bulk food store owners and supermarket packagers. What is the novice bean buyer to think when he/she sees the same pulse (a generic name for edible legumes) labelled a "bean" in one outlet and just down the street it's a "pea"? One bulk food owner confided that she orders them as black-eyed **beans** and puts them in a bin marked black-eyed **peas**! The short answer is yes, they are beans but they don't need presoaking.

1 1/4 cups	dried black-eyed peas	300 mL
3 cups	water	750 mL
1	whole boneless, skinned chicken breast, cut in 1" (2.5 cm) pieces	1
1	large onion, chopped	1
2 Tbsp	vegetable oil	25 mL
3	cloves garlic, minced	3
1	can (28 oz/798 mL) tomatoes, chopped	1
1	green pepper, chopped	1
2 Tbsp	chili powder	25 mL
	salt and pepper to taste	
1/2 tsp	red pepper sauce (optional)	2 mL

■ In large covered pot, simmer the beans in 3 cups of water for 30-40 minutes until soft but not mushy. Do not drain.

■ Meanwhile, in skillet, sauté chicken pieces, onion and garlic in oil until chicken loses pink colour. Add chicken mixture and remaining ingredients to beans. Stir well.

■ Simmer uncovered for 20 minutes. Adjust thickness of mixture by adding more water or tomato juice if necessary. Chili should be "loose" but not "runny" or you have just made another pot of soup!

■ Taste and add salt, pepper and pepper sauce if desired.

Serves 4.

Skillet Chili Chicken

▮▮▮▮▮▮▮▮▮▮▮▮▮▮

A complete meal in a pan. Accompanied by your favourite bread, you're home at 5:30 and sitting down by 6:15, thanks to instant rice and canned beans. It is a mild chili dish, so feel free to add more spice and hot pepper sauce.

1 lb	boneless chicken breasts, cut in 6 pieces	450 g
1 Tbsp	vegetable oil	15 mL
1	medium onion, chopped	1
1	green pepper, chopped	1
3	cloves garlic, minced	3
1	can (19 oz/540 mL) kidney beans, drained	1
1	can (14 oz/398 mL) tomatoes, undrained	1
2 tsp	chili powder	10 mL
3/4 cup	instant rice or 1 cup (250 mL) cooked rice	175 mL
3	dashes, hot pepper sauce (e.g. Tabasco)	3
3/4 cup	Monterey Jack cheese, shredded	175 mL

■ In skillet, lightly brown chicken in oil until pink is no longer evident. Remove and set aside.

■ Add more oil if necessary and sauté onion, pepper and garlic until tender for 5 minutes.

■ Stir in kidney beans, chili powder and tomatoes. Add rice and pepper sauce.

■ Arrange chicken pieces on top of mixture. Cover and simmer for 20 min.

■ Top with shredded cheese and simmer 5 more minutes until cheese melts.

Serves 4.

Moroccan Chicken

*T*here is always a recipe that fights its way to the front of the line, and this is definitely the one. Beloved by all, it can be dressed up or down. For the family, serve over rice. Special occasions demand the exotic twist of raisins and couscous. Easily doubled.

2 Tbsp	**olive oil**	**25 mL**
2	**boneless, skinned chicken breasts, cut in 1/2**	**2**
1	**medium onion, chopped**	**1**
1	**can (14 oz/398 mL) tomatoes, chopped**	**1**
1	**medium zucchini, halved**	**1**
	lengthwise and sliced 1/4" (.5 cm) thick	
1 tsp	**dried oregano**	**5 mL**
2 tsp	**ground cumin (more if desired)**	**10 mL**
1/2 tsp	**ground cinnamon**	**3 mL**
	salt to taste	
1 cup	**canned chick peas, drained and rinsed**	**250 mL**
2 Tbsp	**raisins (optional)**	**25 mL**
11/2 cups	**cooked rice or couscous ***	**375 mL**

* To cook couscous, bring 11/2 cups (375 mL) water to boil in medium saucepan. Add 3/4 cup (175 mL) of couscous, turn off heat, cover, and let stand for 5 minutes. Fluff up with a fork.

■ In skillet, heat oil over medium heat. Brown chicken on both sides. Remove chicken from pan.

■ Add onion and sauté until tender for about 5 minutes. Add tomatoes.

■ Return chicken to skillet and simmer, covered in tomato mixture for 25 to 35 minutes.

■ Stir in zucchini, oregano and spices. Cover and simmer for 5 minutes until zucchini is almost tender.

■ Add chick peas and raisins. Heat through, about 5 minutes.

■ Serve over rice or couscous.

Serves 4.

Salsa Chicken

A busy executive gave us this chicken and kidney bean recipe. Just as good for fish (recipe below) but using black beans.

1	can (19 oz/540 mL) red kidney beans	1
2	boneless, skinned chicken breasts, cut in 1/2	2
1 cup	medium or hot salsa	250 mL

- ■ Drain and rinse kidney beans. Place on the bottom of an ungreased casserole dish.
- ■ Put the four chicken pieces on the beans. Cover with the salsa.
- ■ Bake, covered at 350ºF (180ºC) for 40 minutes.

Serves 4.

Salsa Fish

1	can (15 oz/425 mL) black beans *	1
1¼ lbs	white fish (cod or red snapper are best)	550 g
1 cup	medium or hot salsa	250 mL

* Substitution – 2 cups (500mL) cooked beans

- ■ Drain and rinse black beans. Place on the bottom of an ungreased casserole dish.
- ■ Put the fish on the beans. Cover with the salsa.
- ■ Bake, covered at 350ºF (180ºC) for 15 to 25 minutes depending on the thickness of the fish pieces.

Serves 4.

Quick Spicy Sausage Stew

here are lots of tasty sausages on the market these days. It's up to your palate how much "fire" you can handle. Remember, there's salsa in this recipe as well.

1 lb	spicy sausage, cut in 1/2" (1 cm) slices	450 g
1 Tbsp	vegetable oil	15 mL
1	large onion, chopped	1
2	cloves garlic, minced	2
1	green pepper, chopped	1
1	can (28 oz/796 mL) tomatoes, undrained and chopped	1
1	can (14 oz/398 mL) kidney beans, drained and rinsed	1
1 cup	canned chick peas (garbanzo beans), drained and rinsed	250 mL
1/2 cup	salsa, medium strength	125 mL
1 tsp	ground cumin	5 mL
1 tsp	dried oregano	5 mL

* If using dried, soak and cook 1/2 cup according to directions on pages 9 & 10.

■ In large skillet, brown sausage in oil over medium heat. Remove from pan. Drain fat, leaving a small amount to brown onion and garlic for 5 minutes.

■ Return sausage to pan. Add rest of ingredients, cover and simmer for 20 minutes.

Serves 4-6.

Canadian Cassoulet

The traditional French Cassoulet -- a layered mixture of white beans and meat -- is a complicated recipe. Not many of us have a spare goose or duck in the fridge but it's too good to leave out of our bean cookbook. Our Canadian version is still wonderfully flavourful but much simplified.

2 cups	dried navy or Great Northern beans	500 mL
3	bay leaves	3
1 Tbsp	vegetable oil	15 mL
1/2 lb	each, lamb and pork, cubed	225 g
1/2 lb	garlic sausage, cut in 1/2" (1 cm) slices	225 g
1	onion, chopped	1
2	cloves garlic, minced	2
1	can (19 oz/540 mL) tomatoes, undrained and chopped	1
1 cup	red wine	250 mL
1/2 cup	beef stock *	125 mL
1 tsp	dried thyme (more if desired)	5 mL
1 1/4 cups	fine bread crumbs	300 mL
1/3 cup	fresh parsley, chopped	75 mL

* Can use beef bouillon cubes or instant granules. Follow package directions.

- Soak beans according to quick soak method on page 9. Drain and rinse.
- In large saucepan, place beans and bay leaves. Cover with 2" (5 cm) of water. Bring to boil, reduce heat and simmer for 40 minutes. Drain and rinse.
- While beans are cooking, heat oil in large skillet. Brown meat. Remove from pan. In same pan, lightly brown sausage. Remove from pan.
- Add a little more oil and sauté onions and garlic, about 5 minutes. Add tomatoes, wine and beef stock. Simmer for 5 minutes.
- Return lamb and pork to skillet. Simmer, covered, for 1/2 hour or until tender. Add sausage and thyme. Simmer 5 minutes more.
- In large casserole, layer 1/3 of the beans, then 1/2 the meat mixture. Repeat layers, ending with beans. Add enough liquid (stock or wine) to almost cover beans.
- Make crumb topping by combining bread crumbs and parsley. Bake, uncovered, at 350ºF (180ºC) for 1 hour. Crust will be golden brown. If during the cooking the cassoulet seems to be getting dry, add liquid.

Serves 8-10.

Cowboy Casserole

*An easy, easy, quick, quick dinner casserole. Make it the day before --
keep in the fridge and slip into the oven on returning home. Dieticians
approve of the combination of beans and rice.*

1 lb	ground beef	450 g
1	onion, chopped	1
2	cloves garlic, minced	2
1 tsp	chili powder	5 mL
1	can (28 oz/796 mL) tomatoes, chopped	1
1 cup	uncooked instant rice	250 mL
1	can (14 oz/398 mL) kidney beans, drained and rinsed	1
1 cup	cheddar cheese, grated	250 mL

■ In skillet, brown beef, onion and garlic over medium heat. Drain fat.

■ Transfer mixture to oven proof casserole and stir in remaining ingredients except cheese.

■ Bake, covered, for 40 minutes at 350°F (180°C). Uncover, sprinkle with grated cheese. Return to oven and bake uncovered for 10 minutes more or until cheese is melted.

Serves 4-6.

Robinson Crusoe

*T*his *layered casserole has been in our family for so many years the reason for its name is a mystery. Perhaps the famous castaway had only one pot on the island for cooking dinner.*

2 cups	potatoes, peeled and sliced	500 mL
2 cups	celery, chopped	500 mL
1 lb	ground beef	450 g
1 Tbsp	Worcestershire sauce	15 mL
1/2 tsp each	salt and pepper	3 mL
1	large onion, sliced	1
1	large green pepper, sliced	1
1	can (19 oz/540 mL) kidney beans, drained and rinsed	1
1	can (19 oz/540 mL) tomatoes, chopped	1
1 tsp each	dried thyme and oregano	5 mL

■ In a large casserole, arrange the potatoes on the bottom of the dish. Sprinkle with salt and pepper.

■ Layer the celery followed by a layer of uncooked ground beef. Sprinkle with Worcestershire sauce.

■ Add onions, green pepper and kidney beans in separate layers. Sprinkle with thyme and oregano.

■ Top with the canned tomatoes. Cover and cook at 350ºF (180ºC) for 1-11/2 hours.

Serves 6.

Bean and Veggie Burritos

This recipe uses leftover Baked Black Beans (page 86). You can be as imaginative as you like with the filling.

2 tsp	vegetable oil	10 mL
1	small onion, finely chopped	1
3	cloves garlic, minced	3
1/2	green pepper, thinly sliced	1/2
1/2	red or yellow pepper, thinly sliced	1/2
1	medium zucchini, cut in 1 1/2" (3.5 cm) strips	1
1/2 cup	mushrooms, sliced	125 mL
1 tsp	dried oregano	5 mL
2 tsp	chili powder	10 mL
1 tsp	ground cumin	5 mL
3/4 cup	cooked rice (optional)	175 mL
6	flour tortillas	6
2 cups	Baked Black Beans *	500 mL
1/2 cup	Monterey Jack cheese, grated	125 mL
6 Tbsp	salsa	90 mL
6 Tbsp	low fat sour cream	90 mL

* See page 86 for instructions.

- In skillet, sauté onion in oil over medium heat for 2 minutes. Add garlic and vegetables, cook, stirring often until vegetables are just tender.
- Add oregano, chili and cumin and if desired, hot cooked rice. Mix well.
- While vegetable mixture is cooking, wrap tortillas tightly in foil. Heat in a 350°F (180°C) oven for 10 minutes.
- Take out tortillas. Spread with 1/3 cup (75 mL) of Baked Black Beans and 1/3 cup (75 mL) of vegetable mixture across each tortilla, just below the centre. Top with cheese, salsa and sour cream.
- Fold bottom edge of tortilla over filling, fold in sides and roll up.
- If burritos are not desired temperature, place on a baking sheet, seam side down, and bake at 350°F (180°C) for 10 minutes.
- Serve with additional salsa and sour cream.

Serves 6.

Tortilla Stack

︻▸▸▸▸▸▸▸▸▸▸▸▸▸▸▸▸▸︼

W*e think of this as Mexican lasagne where tortillas replace the pasta. A favourite with teenagers.*

2 tsp	vegetable oil	10 mL
1	small onion, finely chopped	1
1	green pepper, finely chopped	1
1	clove garlic, minced	1
1	jalapeno pepper, minced	1
1 tsp	dried oregano	5 mL
1	can (14 oz/398 mL) tomato sauce	1
11/2 cups	cooked black beans *	375 mL
1/2 cup	kernel corn, canned or fresh (optional) **	125 mL
3 or 4	large tortillas	3 or 4
11/2 cups	grated cheddar or Monterey Jack cheese	375 mL

* If using dried beans, soak and cook 3/4 of a cup (125 mL), following instructions on page 9 and 10.

** If not adding corn, add an extra 1/2 cup of cooked black beans.

■ In large saucepan, sauté onion, green pepper, garlic and jalapeno pepper in oil over medium heat for 5 minutes.

■ Add other ingredients except tortillas and cheese. Simmer, covered for 30 minutes. Add more liquid if getting dry. Mash the bean mixture against the sides of the saucepan to obtain a smoother consistency.

■ Lightly oil an 8"x8" (20cm x 20cm) pan.

■ Cut tortillas in 1" (2.5 cm) strips and place a single layer in the bottom of pan.

■ Spoon on 1/3 of the bean mixture then 1/3 of the cheese. Repeat layers twice.

■ Cover with foil and bake at 375ºF(190ºC) for 25 minutes or until hot. If desired, serve with light sour cream and salsa.

Serves 4.

Mexican Brunch

The perk in taking a Mexican vacation in the middle of writing a cookbook was the discovery of a totally unexpected recipe. Described verbally in a square in Puerto Vallarta, it sounded delicious and so it proved to be.

2	medium tortillas	2
1/2 cup	refried beans *	125 mL
4	eggs	4
1/4 cup	milk	125 mL
2 tsp	butter or margarine	10 mL
	salsa	

* Use canned or make your own. Recipe page 106.

- Place tortillas on baking sheet and cover with refried beans. Warm in 325°F (160°C) oven for 5 to 10 minutes.
- Meanwhile, in medium bowl, beat eggs and milk.
- In skillet, melt butter over low heat. Add eggs and stir frequently until creamy but not dry.
- Spoon scrambled eggs over warm tortillas. Top with salsa.
- Serve immediately.

Serves 2.

Enchiladas

𝕡𝕡𝕡𝕡𝕡𝕡𝕡𝕡𝕡𝕡𝕡𝕡𝕡𝕡

*T*hese are easy to make if you have some Black Bean Chili (page 70) or Baked Black Beans (page 86) on hand to use for filling. We think you'll find them as good as any meat filled enchiladas.

8	medium sized flour tortillas	8
3 cups	Black Bean Chili or Baked Black Beans *	750 mL
	Enchilada Sauce (recipe follows)	
1 cup	cheddar or Monterey Jack cheese, grated	250 mL
Enchilada Sauce:		
2 tsp	vegetable oil	10mL
1	medium onion, finely chopped	1
2	cans (14 oz/398 mL) tomato sauce	2
1/2 cup	water	125 mL
2 tsp	chili powder (more if desired)	10 mL
1/2 tsp	ground cumin (more if desired)	3 mL
1/2 tsp	oregano	3 mL

* *Recipes found on pages 70 and 86.*

- ■ To make sauce, sauté onion in oil in medium saucepan over medium heat for 5 minutes. Add other sauce ingredients, cover and simmer for 30 minutes.

- ■ To assemble: warm enchiladas slightly so they roll more easily. In a lightly oiled 9"x13" (22 x 33cm) pan, cover the bottom with a thin layer of enchilada sauce.

- ■ Put about 1/3 cup (75 mL) of Black Bean Chili in a strip down the middle of a tortilla. Top with 1 Tbsp (15 mL) of cheese. Roll tortilla around filling and place seam side down in a single layer in the baking pan.

- ■ Cover tortillas completely with remaining sauce. Sprinkle with the rest of the cheese. Bake at 350ºF (180ºC) for 20 to 25 minutes.

Makes 8 enchiladas.

Black Bean Cornmeal Casserole

*T*his *richly coloured casserole will satisfy any hungry person's appetite.
Not only a crowd pleaser, but the real plus is that it takes only a few
minutes to assemble. Serve with a tossed salad.*

1 cup	**cooked black beans ***	**250 mL**
1 Tbsp	**olive oil**	**15 mL**
1	**medium onion, chopped**	**1**
1	**can (14 oz/398 mL) kernel corn, drained**	**1**
1	**can (19 oz/540 mL) tomatoes, chopped**	**1**
1	**can (4 oz/114 mL) diced green**	**1**
	chilies, drained	
1 cup	**cornmeal**	**250 mL**
1 tsp	**baking powder**	**5 mL**
1 tsp	**baking soda**	**5 mL**
2 tsp	**chili powder**	**10 mL**
1¼ cup	**milk**	**300 mL**
½ cup	**cheddar cheese, grated**	**125 mL**

* Can use drained and rinsed canned black beans

■ If using dried black beans, soak and cook 1/2 cup (125 mL) according to
directions on pages 9 and 10.

■ In skillet, sauté onions in oil over medium heat for 5 minutes.

■ In large bowl, combine onions and other ingredients, except cheese. Mix well.
Place in a lightly oiled 8" x8" (20 cm x 20 cm) baking pan. Top with grated
cheese.

■ Bake, uncovered, at 350ºF (180ºC) for 45 minutes.

Serves 6.

Baked Black Beans

Black beans have now elbowed navy beans off centre stage. This casserole is the '90s answer to your grandmother's Boston Baked Bean recipe. Make lots so it can be used in your quesadillas and burritos.

2 cups	dried black beans	500 mL
1/4 lb	bacon, cut in narrow strips (optional)	100 g
2 Tbsp	vegetable oil	25 mL
1	large green pepper, chopped	1
1	large onion, chopped	1
3	cloves garlic, minced	3
1	can (4 oz/114 mL) diced green chilies	1
1/2 cup	sherry *	125 mL
1 Tbsp	ground cumin	15 mL
1	can (14 oz/398 mL) tomato sauce	1
1/4 cup	fresh cilantro, finely chopped	50 mL

* Red wine can be substituted.

- Soak beans using quick soak method page 9. Drain and rinse.
- In large saucepan, place beans and cover with 3" (7.5 cm) water. Bring to boil, reduce heat, cover and simmer until tender, about 30 minutes. Drain and rinse.
- In skillet, cook bacon until crisp. Remove from pan. Drain fat.
- In the same skillet, add oil and sauté green pepper, onion and garlic until tender, about 5 minutes.
- Place all ingredients in a large casserole and bake covered at 325ºF (160ºC) for 1 hour. Check occasionally and add liquid if necessary.

Serves 6.

Many Baked Beans

*T*his recipe could also be called the NAFTA Casserole. Representative beans from Canada, Mexico and the U.S.A. are all in the same pot simmering together. Hopefully NAFTA's results will be as satisfying as this dish.

1/2 cup	dried navy beans	125 mL
1/2 cup	dried black beans	125 mL
1/2 cup	dried kidney beans or small red beans	125 mL
1/2 cup	dried pinto beans	125 mL
1/4 lb	bacon, cut in match stick pieces	100 g
2	medium onions, chopped	2
1	green pepper, chopped	1
1 tsp	ground allspice	5 mL
2 Tbsp	light molasses	25 mL
2 Tbsp	brown sugar	25 mL
1 Tbsp	tomato ketchup	15 mL
1 tsp	dry mustard	5 mL
1 Tbsp	soy sauce	15 mL
1	can (14 oz/398 mL) tomato sauce	1
1cup	water	250 mL
	juice of one lemon	

■ Combine beans. Rinse. Soak beans using quick soak method on page 9. Drain.

■ In large saucepan, place beans and cover with 3" (7.5 cm) water. Bring to boil, reduce heat, cover and simmer for 40 minutes. Drain and rinse.

■ While beans are cooking, fry bacon in a large skillet until crisp. Remove from skillet. Sauté onions and green pepper in bacon fat for 5 minutes.

■ Add bacon and remaining ingredients. Simmer for 5 minutes more.

■ In large lightly greased casserole, combine beans and tomato mixture.

■ Bake covered at 325ºF (160ºC) for 1 to 1½ hours, checking occasionally and adding liquid if necessary.

Serves 6.

Quick Southern Pizza

A *change of taste from the usual pizza. Can be assembled in five minutes if you use the pre-made bread shells or pizza crusts featured in supermarkets. The sauce can be kept in the fridge for at least a week and freezes well.*

Black Bean Sauce *:		
1	can (14 oz/398 mL) black beans, drained and rinsed **	1
1	can (4 oz/114 mL) green chilies, undrained	1
1 tsp	chicken flavoured granules	5 mL
1	clove garlic, minced	1
1/2 tsp	ground cumin	3 mL
	pizza crust, your choice of size	

*Can also use Black Bean Hummus as the base, page 21.
** If you are starting with dried beans, soak and cook 3/4 cup (125 mL) according to directions on pages 9 and 10.

■ Combine beans and undrained chilies in blender or food processor. Whirl for a few seconds. Add rest of ingredients and blend until smooth. Use immediately or keep in fridge to use as a base for your pizzas.

Yield: 1 1/2 cups (375 mL)

■ First, spread the black bean sauce mixture generously over the pizza and top with any of the following:

Suggested Topping Combinations:

1. Shrimp, chopped green onions, crumbled feta cheese.
2. Sliced mushrooms, diced canned green chilies, grated Havarti or Cheddar cheese.
3. Chopped, seeded tomatoes, green pepper, grated Monterey Jack.

■ Bake in the oven following the pizza crust directions.

Mexican Lentil Casserole

*E*ven *if lentils have not been your favourite food, we feel you will be won over by this recipe. No problem with leftovers, use them for filling burritos or quesadillas.*

2 Tbsp	vegetable oil	25 mL
1	medium onion, chopped	1
1	medium green pepper, chopped	1
3	stalks celery, chopped	3
4 cups	water	1 L
1 cup	dried green/brown lentils	250 mL
11/2 cups	cooked rice (brown is nice)	375 mL
1	can (5.5 oz/156 mL) tomato paste	1
1	pkg (11/4 oz/39 mL) taco seasoning mix	1
1 tsp	chili powder, more if desired	5 mL
1/2 cup	crushed taco chips (optional)	125 mL
1/2 cup	cheddar or Monterey Jack cheese, grated	125 mL

- In large saucepan, sauté onions, green peppers and celery in oil over medium heat for 5 minutes.

- Add water and bring to boil. Stir in lentils. Cover, reduce heat and simmer for 40 minutes. Do not drain.

- In medium sized, lightly oiled casserole, combine lentils with other ingredients except taco chips and cheese. Bake uncovered for 20 minutes at 350°F (180°C).

- Sprinkle taco chips and cheese on top. Bake another 5 minutes or until cheese is melted.

Serves 6.

Self-Crusting Lentil Quiche

*A*s the name suggests, you are saved the trouble of making a separate crust. Complete the meal with a green salad and Dilly Crisps, page 115 in the Bread section.

1/2 cup	dried green/brown lentils	125 mL
1/2 tsp	savory	3 mL
1 Tbsp	vegetable oil	15 mL
1	medium onion, chopped	1
2	cloves garlic, minced	2
1 Tbsp	lemon juice	15 mL
	freshly ground pepper	
3	eggs	3
1 cup	milk (can use skim)	250 mL
1/4 tsp	salt	1 mL
1 tsp	dried basil	5 mL
1 tsp	dried oregano	5 mL
1/2 cup	all purpose flour	125 mL
1/2 tsp	baking powder	3 mL
1/2 cup	medium cheddar cheese, grated	125 mL
3	tomatoes, thinly sliced	3
2 Tbsp	freshly grated parmesan cheese	25 mL

- Rinse lentils. Place in medium saucepan with 2 cups (500 mL) water and savory. Simmer, covered for 25 minutes. Drain.

- In skillet, sauté onions and garlic in oil over medium heat for 5 minutes or until tender. Remove from heat and add lemon juice and black pepper to taste.

- In large bowl, beat together eggs, milk, salt and herbs. Stir in flour and grated cheese, but don't overmix.

- Combine lentils with cooked onion mixture. Stir into batter. Pour into 9" greased **metal*** pie, cake or flan pan (at least 11/4"/ 3.5 cm high).

- Top with tomato slices, then sprinkle with parmesan cheese.

- Bake 25 to 30 minutes at 425°F (220°C) or until centre is firm when pressed.

* Must use a metal pan.

Serves 6 for lunch or 4 for dinner.

Italian Pasta & Beans

There are many recipes for this traditional Italian dish, Paste e Fagioli. This is ours -- quick and inexpensive. Suggested accompaniment, Garlic Buns, page 114 in the Bread section.

3 Tbsp	olive oil	45 mL
2	cloves garlic, minced	2
1	can (19 oz/540 mL) tomatoes, chopped	1
1/2 cup	fresh parsley, chopped	125 mL
1 tsp	dried basil	5 mL
1 tsp	dried oregano	5 mL
	salt and pepper to taste	
1 cup	cooked white kidney beans *	250 mL
1 cup	penne or elbow pasta	250 mL
	parmesan cheese	

* If using dried beans, prepare 1/2 cup (125 mL) according to soaking and cooking instructions on pages 9 and 10.

- Cook pasta according to package directions. Keep warm.
- In medium saucepan, sauté garlic in oil over medium heat for 2 minutes. Add tomatoes, parsley, basil and oregano. Simmer for 15 minutes, breaking up the tomatoes.
- Add beans and simmer for 5 minutes. Taste and add salt and pepper as desired.
- Place warm pasta in a heated bowl. Cover with sauce. Toss well.
- Serve with parmesan cheese.

Serves 4.

Veggie Spaghetti Sauce

This family recipe has evolved over the years. Gradually the amount of ground beef has been reduced and veggies have been added. Now chick peas have replaced the ground beef. Double the recipe to make Vegetarian Lasagne, page 93, and have some left for a simple spaghetti dinner. Freezes well.

1 Tbsp	vegetable oil	15 mL
1	large onion, finely chopped	1
2	cloves garlic, minced	2
1	green pepper, chopped	1
1	medium zucchini, chopped	1
1 cup	sliced mushrooms	250 mL
1	can (28 oz/796 mL) crushed tomatoes	1
2	cans (5 1/2 oz/156 mL) tomato paste	2
1	can (19 oz/540 mL) chick peas (garbanzo beans), drained and rinsed	1
1 cup	water	250 mL
1 cup	red wine *	250 mL
1 tsp	paprika	5 mL
1 tsp	dried basil	5 mL
1 tsp	dried oregano	5 mL
1/2 tsp	thyme	3 mL
1/2 tsp	allspice	3 mL
8 drops	hot red pepper sauce (e.g. Tabasco)	8 drops
	salt and pepper to taste	

* Can substitute water or stock, but wine is the best.

■ In soup pot, sauté onion, garlic and green pepper in oil over medium heat for 5 minutes. Add zucchini and mushrooms. Cook 3 minutes more.

■ Add tomatoes, tomato paste, chick peas and liquid. Simmer partially covered for 40 minutes. Stir occasionally.

■ Add herbs and spices and cook 15 minutes more.

■ Serve over cooked spaghetti. Sprinkle with freshly grated parmesan cheese.

Yields 6 cups.

Vegetarian Lasagne

*D*o *you hesitate to make lasagne because it is too time consuming? With spaghetti sauce on hand and the new on-the-market oven ready lasagne noodles, it takes less than 15 minutes to assemble. Nice served with Herb Bread, page 116 in the Bread Section.*

8 cups	**Veggie Spaghetti Sauce, page 92**	**1.5 L**
	(double recipe, reserve 4 cups for future use)	
12	**oven ready lasagne noodles ***	**12**
10 oz	**mozzarella cheese**	**300 g**
16 oz	**light cottage cheese**	**500 g**
1	**egg, beaten**	**1**
1/2 cup	**parmesan cheese, grated**	**125 mL**

* Can use fresh if available. Just ask for enough to make 3 layers.

- Thinly slice mozzarella cheese.
- In bowl, blend cottage cheese and eggs.
- In a deep 9"x13" (22 x 33cm) baking dish, spread a thin layer of spaghetti sauce. Arrange a layer of lasagne noodles, placed lengthwise over sauce. Spread one third of the remaining sauce over noodles, then a second layer of lasagne noodles placed widthwise.
- Cover with all the cottage cheese mixture and half the mozzarella cheese slices then another third of the meat sauce.
- Place the final layer of lasagne noodles lengthwise, cover with remainder of the meat sauce and the rest of the mozzarella cheese slices.
- Sprinkle with parmesan cheese.
- Bake at 350ºF (180ºC) for 40 minutes. Let stand for 10 minutes before serving.

Serves 8.

Fettucine with Vegetables

*B*eans and pasta discover each other. The result -- a main dish that will aid an out-of-whack entertaining budget. It's pasta primavera with a crunch!

1 lb	fettucine	450 g
2 tsp	olive oil	10 mL
1	large red pepper, cut in 11/2" (3.5cm) strips	1
1	clove garlic, minced	1
1	zucchini, cut in 11/2" (3.5cm) strips	1
3	green onions, chopped	3
2 Tbsp	butter or margarine	25 mL
2 tsp	lemon juice	10 mL
1/2 tsp	grated lemon rind	3 mL
2 tsp	Dijon mustard	10 mL
1/3 cup	chicken stock *	75 mL
11/2 cups	canned chick peas (garbanzo beans), drained and rinsed	375 mL
3 Tbsp	fresh parsley, chopped	45 mL
1/2 tsp	dried basil	3 mL
	salt and pepper to taste	

* Can use bouillon cubes or instant granules. Follow package instructions.

■ In skillet, sauté red pepper and garlic in oil over medium heat for 3 minutes. Add zucchini and green onions and cook 2 minutes more. Remove vegetables from pan.
■ Melt butter in skillet. Add lemon juice, rind, mustard and chicken stock. Stir.
■ Add vegetables, chick peas, basil and parsley. Heat for 5 minutes.
■ While making sauce, cook fettucine in boiling water until tender, following package directions. Drain.
■ Add sauce to fettucine. Toss and heat through.
■ Serve on warmed plates. Sprinkle with parmesan cheese.

Serves 4.

Yellow Split Pea Dal

Dal is a traditional Indian dish and this is one of the many variations. It is a prime source of protein in India. A plus is that it reheats well.

1 Tbsp	vegetable oil	15 mL
1	medium onion, chopped	1
2	cloves garlic, minced	2
2	medium carrots, chopped	2
3/4 cup	dried yellow split peas	175 mL
11/2 cups	chicken stock*	375 mL
1 tsp	turmeric	5 mL
1 tsp	chili powder	5 mL
11/2 tsp	ground ginger	8 mL
1/2 tsp	coriander	3 mL
1	medium zucchini, cut in 1/2" (1 cm) cubes	1
1 cup	canned crushed tomatoes	250 mL
2 cups	hot cooked brown rice	500 mL
11/2 cups	hot cooked broccoli (optional)	375 mL

* Can use chicken bouillon cube or instant granules.

■ In a large saucepan, sauté onion, garlic and carrots in oil over medium heat until tender, about 5 minutes.

■ Add split peas, stock and spices. Reduce heat, cover and simmer 45 minutes.

■ Add zucchini and tomatoes and simmer for another 20 minutes, stirring occasionally.

■ On individual serving plates, mound rice. Place broccoli on the rice and spoon dal mixture over both. Serve with yogurt and chopped cilantro if desired.

Serves 4.

Chick Pea Curry

The friend who gave us this recipe said, "you can curry almost anything" and she did as she stretched her budget to feed her family of eight. Here is a vegetarian adaptation made with chick peas. It is important to use a good quality Indian curry powder.

2 Tbsp	vegetable oil	25 mL
1	large onion, finely chopped	1
1 Tbsp	curry powder (more if desired)	15 mL
2 Tbsp	flour	25 mL
2 cups	stock - vegetable or chicken *	500 mL
1/2 cup	raisins	125 mL
1/4 cup	fine coconut **	50 mL
1	apple, peeled and grated	1
1 tsp	tomato ketchup	5 mL
1 tsp	sugar	5 mL
1 tsp	Worcestershire sauce	5 mL
1	can (19 oz/540 mL) chick peas	1
	(garbanzo beans), drained and rinsed	
1 1/2 cups	cooked rice (long grain converted is nice)	375 mL

* Can use bouillon cubes or instant granules. Follow package directions.

** You can use 1/4 cup (50 mL) coconut milk instead.

- In deep skillet, sauté onion in oil over medium heat until tender, about 5 minutes. Stir in curry powder and flour.
- Add stock slowly, stirring constantly.
- Add all other ingredients, except chick peas and rice. Simmer for 15 to 20 minutes. Adjust seasoning.
- Add chick peas and heat through, about 5 minutes.
- Serve over cooked rice. Chutney is a great accompaniment.

Serves 4.

Spicy Vegetable Medley

This tempting mix of vegetables and chick peas makes a delicious side dish or a full meal served over rice.

2 Tbsp	vegetable oil	25 mL
1	medium onion, chopped	1
1	clove garlic, minced	1
1 Tbsp	curry powder	15 mL
1 tsp	ground cumin	5 mL
1/4 tsp	ground allspice	2 mL
1 tsp	ground ginger	5 mL
1	can (4 oz/114 mL) diced green chilies	1
1 Tbsp	flour *	15 mL
2 cups	vegetable or chicken stock **	500 mL
2	medium carrots, chopped	2
2	medium potatoes, chopped	2
1/2	small cauliflower, chopped	1/2
1 cup	green beans, cut in 1" (2.5 cm) slices	250 mL
1	medium apple, peeled and chopped	1
1	can (19 oz/540 mL) chick peas (garbanzo beans) drained and rinsed	1

* *If serving as vegetable, use 1 cup (250 mL) stock and 1 1/2 tsp (8 mL) flour.*

** *Can use bouillon cubes or instant granules. Follow package directions.*

■ In skillet, sauté onion in oil over medium heat for 5 minutes. Add garlic, curry powder, spices and green chilies. Stir for 2 minutes more.

■ Add flour and blend for 1 minute. Gradually stir in stock. Continue to stir until mixture boils and thickens slightly.

■ Add vegetables. Cover and simmer for about 10 minutes until vegetables are tender.

■ Add apples and chick peas and heat through.

■ Serve over cooked brown rice or your favourite pasta.

Serves 6.

Gratin of White Beans with Herbs

Served with a tossed salad and crusty brown buns, this makes a
satisfying meal. Also can be a side dish with lamb or pork. This recipe
makes a large amount so it can easily be halved.

2 1/2 cups	dried navy or Great Northern beans	625 mL
3 Tbsp	olive oil	45 mL
1	medium onion, chopped	1
2	cloves garlic, minced	2
2	fresh tomatoes, peeled and chopped	2
1/2 cup	chicken stock *	125 mL
1/2 cup	whipping cream (half and half works too)	125 mL
	salt and freshly ground pepper to taste	
Topping:		
1 1/2 cups	bread crumbs	375 mL
2	green onions, finely chopped	2
1/3 cup	butter or margarine, melted	75 mL
2 tsp	dried rosemary **	10 mL
2 tsp	dried thyme **	10 mL
1/3 cup	fresh parsley, chopped	75 mL

* Can use chicken bouillon cubes or instant granules. Follow package directions.

** Use fresh if available, but remember to use 3 times as much.

- Soak beans using quick soak method on page 9. Drain and rinse.

- In large saucepan, cover beans with water. Cover and cook over low heat until tender, about 45 minutes. Drain and rinse.

- In skillet, sauté onion and garlic in oil over medium heat for 5 minutes. Add tomatoes and cook 10 minutes more, stirring frequently.

- Add stock, cream, salt and pepper and stir another 2 minutes.

- In large lightly oiled casserole, place beans and stir in other ingredients.

- Mix topping ingredients together and sprinkle on bean mixture. Bake at 375°F (190°C), uncovered, for 30 minutes.

Serves 8.

More Bean Favourites

VEGETABLES & SIDE DISHES

Vegetables & Side Dishes

Broccoli & Chick Peas

*T*he nutty flavour of chick peas, combined with broccoli, makes a novel pairing. Most people don't realize that you only need to cut the bottom inch off the broccoli stalk. Peel the rest of the stem – it's all usable.

1 Tbsp	vegetable oil	15 mL
5	medium stalks broccoli, stems peeled	5
	and sliced, heads cut into small florets	
3 Tbsp	water	45 mL
1	can (19 oz/540 mL) chick peas,	1
	drained and rinsed	
1/2 cup	canned artichoke hearts, chopped	125 mL
2 Tbsp	oil from artichokes	25 mL
2 tsp	fine herbs	10 mL
4-6	sun dried tomatoes, cut in strips (optional)	4-6

■ In skillet or wok, heat oil over medium heat. Add broccoli and stir-fry for 3 to 5 minutes.

■ Add water and cover. Cook for about 3 minutes (broccoli should still be a little crunchy).

■ Add other ingredients and heat through.

Serves 6.

Zucchini Garbanzo Stir-fry

*S*erve with cold ham or chicken and Poppy Seed Fingers, page 113 in the Bread section. Most economical when your friends start presenting you with their excess produce in September. Cut those large zucchinis in chunks.

1	red onion, sliced in rings	1
2	small zucchinis, cut in 1/4" (.5 cm) slices	2
1 Tbsp	vegetable oil	15 mL
1	large fresh tomato, chopped	1
1 cup	canned garbanzo beans (chick peas), drained and rinsed	250 mL
1 tsp	dried thyme	5 mL
1 tsp	dried basil	5 mL
	salt and pepper to taste	

■ In skillet, sauté onion and zucchini in oil over medium heat for 3 minutes.

■ Stir in tomatoes, garbanzo beans, basil and thyme.

■ Cover and simmer 15 minutes or until zucchini is tender.

■ Taste and adjust seasonings.

Serves 4.

Bean Counter's Medley

Accountants would give the nod to investing in this vegetable dish for company. The bottom line is lots of value for your money -- the extra dividend -- delicious!

1	can (14 oz/398 mL) crushed tomatoes	1
1/4 cup	vinegar	50 mL
1/2 cup	tomato ketchup	125 mL
1 cup	celery, chopped	250 mL
1	large onion, cut in rings	1
1	green pepper, cut in strips	1
1	can (19 oz/540 mL) kidney beans	1
1	can (14 oz/398 mL) lima beans	1
1	can (14 oz/398 mL) cut green beans *	1
1	can (14 oz/398 mL) cut yellow beans	1
1	can (14 oz/398 mL) baked beans, undrained	1

* Can use 10 oz (300 g) package of frozen green beans.

- In large casserole, combine crushed tomatoes, vinegar and ketchup.
- Add onions, green pepper and celery.
- Drain liquid from all the beans except baked beans. Add all beans to casserole mixture. Stir well.
- Bake covered in 350ºF (180ºC) oven for 45 minutes.

Serves 8-10.

IN CASE OF HUNGER BREAK CONTAINER!

Stuffed Baked Potatoes

Y*ou only need 1/4 cup (50mL) of black beans for this recipe so hopefully you have frozen, cooked ones tucked away. For a light supper, a green salad is all that is needed. Add either baked chicken or a broiled steak if hunger demands.*

4	medium baking potatoes, scrubbed	4
3	stalks broccoli	3
1 Tbsp	olive oil	15 mL
1/2	red pepper, chopped	1/2
1	small zucchini, cut in quarters lengthwise and sliced	1
8	medium mushrooms, sliced	8
1 tsp	ground cumin	5 mL
1 Tbsp	butter or margarine	15 mL
2 Tbsp	plain yogurt	25 mL
1/4 cup	cooked black beans	50 mL
1/3 cup	cheddar or Monterey Jack cheese, shredded	75 mL

- Bake potatoes for 1 hour at 400ºF (200ºC) or until tender.
- While potatoes are baking, wash and peel broccoli stems and slice. Cut florets into small pieces.
- In skillet, heat oil over medium heat. Sauté broccoli and red peppers for 5 minutes.
- Add zucchini and mushrooms. Sauté about 5 minutes more or until vegetables are tender.
- When potatoes are done, cut in half lengthwise. Remove the insides leaving 1/4" (.5 cm) on the skin. Put the rest in a bowl. Mash and add butter, yogurt, cumin, beans and vegetables.
- Place potato cases in a 13" x 9" (22 x 33 cm) baking pan. Spoon vegetable mixture into potato cases. Top with cheese.
- Bake for 10 minutes at 350ºF (180ºC) until cheese melts.

Serves 4 generously.

Tomato Lima Bean Parmigiana

*O*ur recipe card for this one is dog-earred and spotted. Can also be used as a main dish if you double the amount of bacon. Serve with ham and a baked potato for maximum oven use.

4	strips bacon, cut in 1/2" (1 cm) slices	4
1	onion, chopped finely	1
1	can (14 oz/398 mL) lima beans, drained and rinsed *	1
2	cloves garlic, minced	2
1 cup	water	250 mL
2	medium tomatoes, chopped	2
1/2 cup	grated parmesan cheese	125 mL

* Can use 1 package (350 g) frozen lima beans.

■ In skillet, cook bacon over medium heat until crisp. Remove from pan and pat with paper towel to remove excess fat.

■ In ovenproof casserole, combine all ingredients except cheese.

■ Sprinkle cheese on top. Bake uncovered at 325ºF (160ºC) for 25 minutes or until bubbly.

Serves 4.

Bean Bonus

Use the above recipe or any bean and rice mixture to stuff green or red peppers. Slice pepper vertically for a different look.

Curried Cauliflower with Beans

*T*ired of cauliflower with cheese sauce? This is an unlikely combination
of flavours and colours, but it works!

1/2 tsp	ground ginger	3 mL
2	cloves garlic, minced	2
1 Tbsp	vegetable oil	15 mL
1	cauliflower, cut in florets	1
2	tomatoes, finely chopped	2
2 Tbsp	lime juice	25 mL
1 tsp	curry powder	5 mL
3 Tbsp	water	45 mL
1 cup	red kidney beans, drained and rinsed	250 mL

■ In a medium saucepan, sauté garlic and ginger in oil over medium heat for 2 minutes.

■ Stir in tomatoes, lime juice, curry powder and water. Simmer for 3 minutes.

■ Add cauliflower, cover and simmer over medium heat for 8 minutes.

■ Add beans. Stir and heat thoroughly.

■ Taste and adjust seasonings.

Serves 4-6.

White Beans Provence

This recipe is an attempt to come close to a delicious bean dish served with lamb shanks in a Napa Valley restaurant. It's hard to dissect a dish under the critical eye of the waiter, but this one was worth it. Excellent as a side dish for any meat.

1 Tbsp	olive oil	15 mL
1	medium onion, chopped	1
1/2 cup	celery, finely chopped	125 mL
2	medium tomatoes, finely chopped	2
2 cups	cooked white beans *	500 mL
1 cup	chicken stock **	250 mL
1 tsp	dried thyme	5 mL
2 Tbsp	fresh parsley, finely chopped	25 mL
	salt and pepper to taste	

* *Soak and cook 1 cup (250mL) dried according to directions on page 9 and 10.*

** *Can use chicken bouillon or instant granules. Follow package directions.*

■ In saucepan, sauté onion and celery in oil over medium heat for 5 minutes.

■ Add rest of ingredients except parsley. Simmer, covered, for 20 minutes, stirring occasionally.

■ Add parsley and salt and pepper. Cook 5 minutes more.

Serves 6.

Refried Beans

■■■■■■■■■■■■■

A bean book wouldn't be complete without a recipe for refried beans. They are served as a side dish with many Mexican meals but can also be used as a filling for burritos or spread on tortillas.

1 cup	dried pinto or red beans *	250 mL
1	bay leaf	1
1	dried red chili	1
3 Tbsp	vegetable oil or bacon fat	45 mL
1	medium onion, chopped	1
2	cloves garlic, minced	2
1	tomato, peeled and chopped finely	1
1 1/2 tsp	ground cumin	8 mL
1/2 tsp	salt	2 mL
	freshly ground pepper	

* Can use 14 oz/398 mL can of beans. Do not drain. Add dried red chili and omit steps one and two.

■ Soak beans using quick soak method, page 9.

■ In large saucepan, place beans, bay leaf, red chili in 1 inch (2.5 cm) of water. Bring to boil, cover and simmer for 35 to 45 minutes until beans are soft. Check during cooking to be sure the beans are not dry. If necessary, add a little more water. Do not drain.

■ Purée undrained beans in food processor or blender.

■ While beans are cooking, in skillet, sauté onion and garlic in oil over medium heat for 5 minutes. Add tomato, cumin, salt and pepper and cook for 5 minutes more.

■ Add puréed beans, a little at a time, to onion mixture, stirring after each addition. Add a little more oil if necessary to give a thick, creamy paste.

Yields 2 cups (500 mL).

Black Beans & Rice

*P*erk up white rice with the addition of beans. The vinegar gives it an extra tang.

1	can (15 oz/425 mL) black beans, drained	1
	and rinsed, or 13/4 cups cooked *	
1 Tbsp	vegetable oil	15 mL
2	cloves garlic, minced	2
1/2	green pepper, chopped	1/2
1/2 tsp	dried oregano	3 mL
3 Tbsp	white vinegar	45 mL
11/2 cups	rice	375 mL

* If using dried beans, prepare 3/4 cup (175 mL) according to soaking and cooking instructions on pages 9 and 10.

■ Cook rice according to package directions.

■ In skillet, sauté pepper and garlic in oil over medium heat for 3 minutes or until just soft.

■ Turn off heat and stir beans, oregano and vinegar into skillet mixture.

■ When rice is ready, add bean mixture to it. Heat through.

Serves 6.

Caribbean Rice

This is an adaptation of a traditional Caribbean dish. A treat for lovers of spicy food. Mates well with grilled white fish.

11/4 cups	dried black-eyed peas	300 mL
2 tsp	vegetable oil	10 mL
1	small red pepper, chopped	1
1	medium onion, chopped	1
3	cloves garlic, minced	3
3	ripe tomatoes, chopped	3
1/2 cup	uncooked white rice (preferably converted)	125 mL
1 cup	chicken stock *	250 mL
1/2 cup	pitted black olives, chopped	125 mL
1/2 tsp	ground allspice	3 mL
1/2 tsp	freshly ground pepper	3 mL
1/4 tsp	cayenne pepper	1 mL
	salt to taste	
2	green onions, chopped (optional)	2

* Can use bouillon cubes or instant granules. Follow package instructions.

- Cook black-eyed peas in 3 cups (750 mL) water for 25 to 30 minutes. Drain.
- In deep skillet, sauté red pepper, onion and garlic in oil over medium heat for 5 minutes.
- Add tomatoes and rice, stir for 1 minute.
- Add remaining ingredients, except green onions, and simmer covered until rice is cooked, about 20 minutes. Add a little more stock if mixture gets too dry.
- Add green onions and stir gently.

Serves 6.

Red Beans & Rice

A *very popular New Orleans dish. Too nourishing not to be enjoyed north of the 49th.*

1 cup	cooked kidney beans or	250 mL
	small red Mexican beans *	
3/4 cup	brown rice	175 mL
2 tsp	vegetable oil	10 mL
1	onion, chopped	1
2	cloves garlic, minced	2
1/2	green pepper, chopped	1/2
1	can (14 oz/398 mL) tomatoes, chopped	1
1	bay leaf	1
1 tsp	dried basil	5 mL
4	drops hot pepper sauce (e.g. Tabasco)	4
	salt and pepper to taste	

* If using dried beans, prepare 1/2 cup (125 mL) according to soaking and cooking instructions on pages 9 and 10.

- Cook brown rice according to package directions.
- In skillet, sauté onion, garlic and green pepper in oil over medium heat for 5 minutes.
- Add beans, tomatoes and rest of the ingredients, except rice. Simmer 15 minutes.
- Place cooked rice in warm bowl. Pour bean mixture over. Can also be served in individual portions.

Serves 4-6.

More Bean Favourites

More Bean Favourites

BREADS

Breads

Gramma's Corn Bread

*H*aving a grandmother from Arkansas gives you a head start in an appreciation for good wholesome food. She never cooked with a recipe, of course, so this is as close as we can get to her cornmeal bread -- the black pepper gives it an extra zip.

3/4 cup	all purpose flour	175 mL
3/4 cup	yellow cornmeal	175 mL
1 Tbsp	sugar	15 mL
1 Tbsp	baking powder	15 mL
1/2 tsp	salt	2 mL
1/2 tsp	freshly ground pepper	2 mL
3/4 cup	milk (can use skim)	175 mL
1	egg	1
2 Tbsp	butter or margarine, melted	25 mL

- Preheat oven to 400ºF (200ºC).
- Lightly grease an 8"x8" (20 cm x 20 cm) pan.
- In large bowl, mix dry ingredients. In separate small bowl, mix milk, egg and melted butter together.
- Pour milk mixture over dry ingredients and stir gently until just moistened. Do no overmix.
- Spoon batter into prepared pan. Bake about 15 minutes or until a toothpick inserted in the centre comes out clean. To serve, cut in squares.

Serves 6-8.

Blue Cheese Poppy Seed Bread

A very filling accompaniment -- definitely for guests. Serve it when the rest of the meal is not too hearty. The illustrations below for cutting the bread should make it clear.

1	loaf, white or brown unsliced bread	1
4 oz	blue cheese (more if you have it)	100 g
1/3 cup	soft margarine or butter	75 mL
3 Tbsp	poppy seeds *	45 mL

* Check directions for softening poppy seeds in recipe for Poppy Seed Fingers, page 113 .

■ Horizontally slice off the rounded top of the loaf (Figure 1). You will now have a rectangular shape.

Figure 1:

■ Starting at the middle top edge of the bread, slice it lengthwise to the bottom crust but not through. Starting at the top again, make four equal cuts across the bread to the bottom crust but not all the way through (Figures 2 &3). You now have 10 rectangular pieces – 5 on either side of the vertical cut (the rest is easy!).

Figure 2:

Lengthwise cut and 4 crosswise cuts.
View looking down at bread.

■ Cream butter and blue cheese well. Spread on all the cut sides. Sprinkle poppy seeds on all cut sides.

Figure 3:

■ Wrap in foil and bake in 350ºF (180ºC) oven for 20-25 minutes. Be sure it is really hot. Serve in a napkin lined bread basket as it can be messy.

Poppy Seed Fingers

*H*ere's a solution for those left-over hot dog buns languishing in your freezer. Why is it a dozen buns and a dozen weiners never come out evenly? Before you start this recipe, please read the hint below.

3	hot dog buns	3
	enough margarine to cover	
1/2 cup	grated parmesan cheese	125 mL
3 Tbsp	poppy seeds *	45 mL

- Heat oven to 400ºF (200ºC).
- Split each bun in half. Cut each half lengthwise into 2 pieces. Lightly butter the cut sides.
- Mix cheese and poppy seeds together in wide, shallow dish. Roll cut surfaces in mixture and place on baking sheet.
- Bake for 7 minutes.

Makes 12 pieces.

*** Hint**: To have more tender and less likely to "stick in you teeth" poppy seeds, place them in a bowl and cover with boiling water. Let sit for 2 hours. Drain excess water. To dry, spread on small pan and bake in a toaster oven at 250ºF (120ºC) until they are pale grey again. The microwave works and so does just leaving them on the counter for a few hours. They do taste better.*

Homemade Melba Toast

Once you've tried the homemade version you will never pluck another package off the store shelves.

1	loaf of thinly sliced brown or white	1
	sandwich bread *	
	softened butter or margarine	

* Some bakeries have a machine to thinly slice bread. Check around. If you are slicing it yourself, slightly frozen bread is easier to use.

- Lightly butter one side of each slice and cut in three strips.
- Place on a cookie sheet and bake at 275ºF (140ºC) for 25 to 35 minutes minutes until lightly browned and crisp.

Yields approximately 60 pieces

Garlic Buns

If our extended families are cursed with orphan buns in the freezer, we feel that this problem could be continent-wide. Mix and match any variety of buns -- they are all happy together.

left-over buns
garlic powder or fresh garlic, minced
butter or margarine.

- Thaw buns and split in half. Mix garlic powder or minced garlic with butter. Amounts depend on how may buns you have and how much you like garlic.
- Place on cookie sheet 6 " (15 cm) under broiler and broil until browned. Keep an eye on them.
- Serve with any of the soups or salads.

Time Management Bread

*F*acilitators at one training centre always share this recipe at the end of the Time Management section. Impress your friends with freshly baked bread even if you work 6 days a week and do your own cleaning. The loaf has a "muffiny" consistency and is not as suitable for sandwiches as it is served with cheese to accompany any of the soup recipes.

3 cups	self-rising flour *	750 mL
3 Tbsp	sugar	45 mL
1	can (12 oz/375 mL) WARM beer	1
3 Tbsp	melted butter or margarine	45 mL

* Keep looking even if you think you can't find it in the flour section. Please don't substitute ordinary flour.

■ Heat oven to 375ºF (190ºC). Grease 9" x 5" (22 x 12 cm) pan.

■ In medium bowl, mix flour and sugar together. Stir in warm beer and beat 60 strokes with a wooden spoon.

■ Pour into pan. Bake 40 minutes.

■ Remove from oven. Drizzle melted margarine over bread. Return to oven and bake for 10 minutes more. Cool and remove from pan.

Serves 8-10.

Herb Bread

*B*est made in the late summer when fresh dill is universally available. Dill is easy to freeze, just snip the heads off and tuck them into a ziploc bag. Then you'll have that fresh taste all year long.

1	large French loaf	1
1/3 cup	fresh parsley, chopped	75 mL
5	green onions, finely chopped	5
2 Tbsp	fresh dill, finely chopped	25 mL
1/4 cup	chives, finely chopped	50 mL
1/2 cup	butter or margarine, softened	125 mL

■ Split bread in half horizontally. In medium bowl, combine chopped herbs with butter. Cream well. Spread mixture on each half of the loaf. Press halves together.

■ Wrap in foil and heat in oven at 350°F (180°C) for 20 to 25 minutes. Open foil and cut vertically in one inch (2.5 cm) slices.

Serves 8

Pita Triangles

*S*imple and quick to make. Serve with any salad or soup that does not have cheese as one of its ingredients. The amount you make is dependent on the number you're catering for.

pita bread, whole wheat or plain
grated cheese (whatever is on hand)

■ Cut pita bread diagonally twice so that each round makes 4 triangles. Open and tuck a little grated cheese in each.

■ Place on baking sheet and bake at 350°F (180°C) for 10 minutes.

Sesame Rounds

*F*rench baguettes are delicious just as they are. However, if you are looking for something a little different or want to use up a slightly stale loaf, here are two ideas.

1	French baguette, cut in 1/2" (1.5 cm) slices	1
	softened butter or margarine	
2-3 Tbsp	sesame seeds	45 mL

■ Spread softened butter on one side of each slice. Sprinkle with sesame seeds.

■ Bake at 400°F (200°C) for 7 to 10 minutes until lightly browned. Can be put under broiler but watch very carefully.

Dilly Crisps

1	French baguette, cut in 1/2" slices	1
	softened butter or margarine	
	fresh dill weed, finely chopped *	

* When dill is not in season it can often be bought fresh in plastic packages in the vegetable section of the market.

■ In small bowl mix butter and dill weed. Spread on one side of baguette slices.

■ Bake at 400°F (200°C) for 7 to 10 minutes or until lightly browned.

Index:

Index

More Bean Favourites

More Bean Favourites

More Bean Favourites

More Bean Favourites

More Bean Favourites

More Bean Favourites

,,,,,,,,,,,,,,,,,

Order Form

Please send me:

_____ copies of **Easy Beans** at $15.00 Cdn (
per book (price includes taxes and shipping)

_____ copies of **More Easy Beans** (our latest be
book) at $15.00 Cdn ($12.00 US) per book (price inc
taxes and shipping)

NUMBER OF BOOKS _____ x $ _____ = _____

Total Enclosed = _____

NAME _____

STREET _____

CITY _____ PROV/STATE _____

POSTAL CODE/ZIP _____ PHONE _____

Please make the cheque or money order payable to Big Bean
Publishing and mail to:

Big Bean Publishing
#201-1508 Mariners Walk
Vancouver, BC Canada V6J 4X9

- ✂ - - - - - - -

Order Form

Please send me:

_____ copies of **Easy Beans** at $15.00 Cdn ($12.00 US)
per book (price includes taxes and shipping)

_____ copies of **More Easy Beans** (our latest bean cookbook) at $15.00 Cdn ($12.00 US) per book (price includes
taxes and shipping)

NUMBER OF BOOKS _____ x $ _____ = _____

Total Enclosed = _____

NAME _____

STREET _____

CITY _____ PROV/STATE _____

POSTAL CODE/ZIP _____ PHONE _____

Please make the cheque or money order payable to Big Bean
Publishing and mail to:

Big Bean Publishing
#201-1508 Mariners Walk
Vancouver, BC Canada V6J 4X9

$12.00 US)

an cook-
ludes